guide pratique
de la communication

Alan CHAMBERLAIN
Professeur à l'université de Nouvelle-Galles du Sud

Ross STEELE
Professeur à l'université de Sydney

100 actes de communication
56 dialogues

Français langue étrangère

Didier

Everyone, that is, apart from Marcus Meldrew, *Hummfff* who's just sitting there looking all grumpy. →

I clear my throat, stand up and avoid EYE contact with Marcus. Here goes...

APPLAUSE

> Hello, everyone. Firstly can I say a HUGE THANK YOU for voting for me.

MORE APPLAUSE

(From the way Marcus is shifting around in his seat and being all awkward, I'm guessing that he didn't vote for me.)

> As one of your NEW school councillors, I promise to do my VERY BEST for ALL of YOU.

Then I hold up my VOTE FOR ME poster.

> Let's make THIS LIST REALLY HAPPEN!

(More cheers - but not from Marcus, who's fed up that HE'S not on the school council.)

I'm **TOP** OF THE CLASS

in the SCHOOL TEST. Sigh...

EVERYTHING is going SO well when there's SUDDENLY a really LOUD noise right next to my HEAD, which gives

me a BIG SHOCK!

There are LOTS of AMAZED faces

staring back at me.

 "That's right, DUDE3 are coming to play

at our school concert. How good is THAT?"

I have to stop speaking because the whole school

has gone completely CRAZY.

Even MARCUS is cheering now.

Norman is leaping around shouting

"YES! YES!" and " DUDE3 !"

I'm waiting for the noise to die down and thinking

about how everything has worked out

SO BRILLIANTLY.

Being voted on to the school council.

DOGZOMBIES supporting DUDE3.

AND...

had the **idea** to contact a $VERY$ special band.

So it's thanks to THEM that I've got $THIS$."

I take out a letter and hold it up so the kids

can see it. "$Shall$ I read $IT?$"

"$YES!$" they shout

(apart from Marcus, who's got his arms folded).

YO! Oakfield School DUDES. We heard you have AWESOME SCHOOL CONCERTS!

I stop reading and say, "They've obviously never been to one of OUR school concerts," which makes everyone "$LAUGH$" (well, not EVERYONE).

We got your FANTASTIC letter and we've decided to come and PLAY at your concert, with the one and only DOGZOMBIES supporting us.

So see you there, little DUDES!

"**WOW**, that's amazing, sir. I wasn't expecting that!" (TESTS aren't my strong point, but I did work EXTRA hard so I'm very pleased about getting a **TOP MARK**.)

As I'm waiting for the kids to stop clapping, I remember something else I want to say.

" " **B**efore I finish I'd like to THANK **AMY PORTER**, who lent me her LUCKY pen."

MORE CLAPPING

AMY LAUGHs and shrugs her shoulders like it was nothing. Marcus looks even more fed up now. (I still ignore him.)

"**N**orman Watson and Derek **F**ingle – both of you, STAND UP!" Derek stands and Norman LEAPS into the air while bowing and smiling at everyone.

"**NOW** I'm a school councillor, I'll be helping with this year's SCHOOL concert, and Norman and Derek

I'm about to finish my speech when Mr Fullerman interrupts me. **"Tom, sorry to stop you, but I have more GOOD NEWS that I'd like to share with the class."**

"More GOOD NEWS, sir? How is that EVEN possible?" I'm joking of course. I can think of LOADS of other things that would be good news, like:

→ MUCH SHORTER school days. GOOD NEWS!

→ DOGZOMBIES becoming the BIGGEST band in the whole world (apart from DUDE3).

GOOD NEWS!

→ Getting a pet. REALLY GOOD NEWS!

I could go on, but Mr Fullerman is waiting... **"Not only have you been voted on to the school council, but you've also achieved the HIGHEST SCORE EVER on last week's test. So congratulations to you, Tom, and VERY WELL DONE!"**

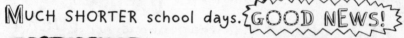

MORE CHEERING AND APPLAUSE

I'm sorry, TOM, did I WAKE you?

(It's Mr Fullerman.)

"No, sir!" I say, quickly opening my ⊙⊙ EYES.
I was having the BEST (daydream) ever, and he's gone
and spoilt it. I'm blinking ⋛⋚ and trying to

THINK of something to say that will

get me out of trouble.

Introducing
NEW
test into
schools
Edition 50

Teachers'
Handbook

"I wasn't asleep, sir. I was ... CONCENTRATING really hard."

"With your eyes CLOSED, Tom?"
Mr Fullerman wonders.

"Yes, sir. I have SPECIAL eyelids that are sort of ... SEE-through. It might LOOK like I was asleep, but I can still tell what's going on even with my eyes closed."

(My dad says that when I change the TV channel while he's asleep.) zzzzzzz ⤵ click

Hey! I was watching that!

"LET me get this right, Tom. You're telling me you have SEE-THROUGH EYELIDS?" Mr Fullerman says while RAISING an eyebrow.

"Yes, sir. Other people in my family have them too."

"That's remarkable. Scientists should be lining up to study your AMAZING eyelids."

"They SHOULD be," I nod.

"But just for NOW could you at least TRY and keep your amazing see-through eyelids ↕ OPEN and your head OFF the desk? That way I'll be able to tell that you're really paying attention in this catch-up class. Is that OK with you, Tom?"

"Yes, sir," I say.

(I'm not sure Mr Fullerman is convinced.)

After he's gone Brad Galloway leans forward and whispers:

"Show me your see-through eyelids, then. That's FREAKY."

"Later, Brad."

(This could take some explaining...)

Somehow I've ended up in **"catch-up class"**.

Being here is SUPPOSED to help me get better marks in my SCHOOL TEST. It's not like I didn't know the answers to the questions; I just wasn't really concentrating as much as I probably should have been. 🙁

The FIRST time Mr Fullerman mentioned the TEST he had his VERY SERIOUS face on. **"Tests are nothing to be nervous about. You just have to work hard and CONCENTRATE. But please don't worry about this**

VERY IMPORTANT TEST."

But the way he kept saying **"VERY IMPORTANT TEST"**

made some kids worry about it a LOT.

(Not me though. )

The school sent a letter home about the TEST that looked quite SERIOUS as well. When Mum and Dad read it, Mum told me,

"Just try your best, Tom. It's not the end of the world if you _don't_ do that well."

"As far as we're concerned it's the EFFORT that really counts. So DON'T worry about the TEST,"

Dad said.

"I'm NOT worried," I said.

Which was TRUE. I wasn't worried at all.

Then Delia turned up and joined in. "So, let me get this STRAIGHT. When Tom comes at the bottom of the class in the TEST, you won't mind?" she said, trying to make a point.

"Tom WON'T be at the bottom of the class. Will you, Tom?" Dad said, looking at me.

"He might be. You're not great at TESTS, are you, Tom?"

"IF Tom IS at the bottom of the class in his TEST - and it's a BIG 'IF' - as long as he's tried his best, we won't mind at all."

I couldn't get a WORD in edgeways with everyone discussing how BADLY I was going to do in this TEST.

EVENTUALLY I managed to say,

"EXCUSE ME!

I might do REALLY WELL in the TEST
and come TOP↑ of the CLASS!"

' '

S I L E N C E.

No one said anything.

FINALLY Mum spoke up and said,

"YES! Of course you might, Tom."

Which made Delia laugh even more.

Ha! Ha! Ha! Ha!

Then she said, "HA! AND guess WHAT? Tom might get a pet UNICORN too. But that's not going to happen, is it?"

"WHAT does THAT mean?"
I wanted to know.

"If you can't say something nice, Delia, just keep QUIET," Mum told her STERNLY.

"You'll be FINE, Tom. Don't worry about a thing," Dad tells me AGAIN.

I could hear Delia still LAUGHING as she went upstairs. Ha! Ha! Ha! Ha! Ha! Ha! Ha! Ha!

Mum and Dad wouldn't stop talking about this TEST even after Delia had left.

Blah Blah "I'm SURE you'll be absolutely fine, as long as you CONCENTRATE," Mum said.

"You do tend to get a bit distracted," Dad added. Then, as they were CHATTING, I suddenly thought of a **VERY** important question.

 "Can I ask you something?"

"Ask away, Tom," Mum and Dad both said patiently.

 "What I <u>REALLY</u> want to know is..."

"YES?"

 "UNICORNS don't ACTUALLY exist, do they?"

SIGH

"No, Tom, they don't."

"I thought so - just checking."

(Mind you, if UNICORNS **DID** exist, how good would THAT be?)

Here are some made-up pets I drew:

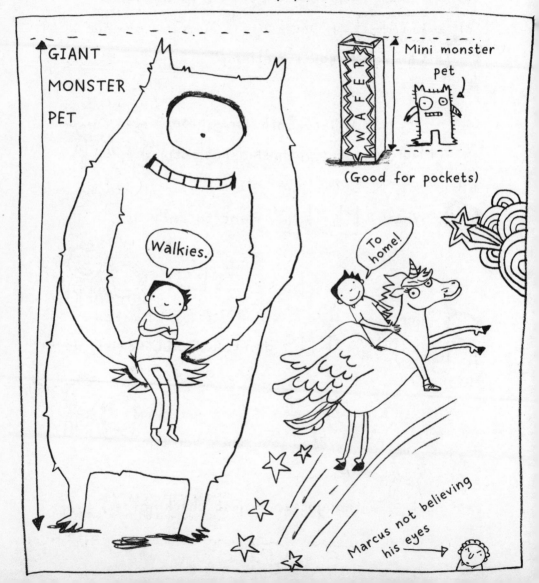

It's not like I DELIBERATELY messed up my TEST. Things just didn't quite work out the way I thought they were going to.

For a START, if Derek 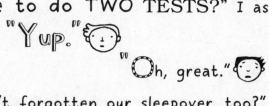 hadn't reminded me about the TEST on the way to school, I'd have forgotten all about it.

TEST... What TEST?

It was written on the calendar but Mum

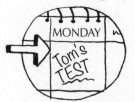
MONDAY
Tom's TEST

and Dad have been EXTRA busy with work so no one reminded me it was today.

"It's a MOCK TEST, not the REAL one," Derek said as we kept walking.

"We have to do TWO TESTS?" I asked.

"Yup."

"Oh, great."

"You haven't forgotten our sleepover, too?" Derek checked with me.

"AS IF."

(We have plans to write some DOGZOMBIES tunes with Norman. 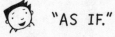 So I was looking forward to THAT.)

Here's what I did BEFORE the TEST

(Which didn't HELP much.)

Mr Fullerman told us we'd start the TEST AFTER our break and we could read until then, which I did for a bit until I got an idea for a drawing.

But I still kept thinking about the TEST.

AGH!

No!

TEST

No test

I thought about it at break time as well. → Test.

It took Norman to say, "Who wants to try on my glasses?" for me to STOP① thinking about it (for a while).

Derek looked like a newsreader when he put them on. Solid's BIG head made the glasses look a lot smaller, and they made my eyes go all FUZZY.

Where are you all?

Here! ((ᴡᴡ))

What I saw looking at Derek

"What would you do if you lost your glasses?" I asked Norman as I handed them back. (Glasses marks)

"Bump into things."

(Or in this case ... Solid.)

When break was over and we went back to class, Mr Fullerman had already put the TEST papers on to our desks.

"Oh, here we go," I whispered. — Groan

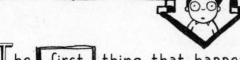

Here's what HAPPENED DuRING the TEST

The **first** thing that happened was Marcus said I had WEIRD marks on my face.

"They're on your nose too."

"I tried on Norman's glasses – maybe it's that. My eyes are still FUZZY," I tried to explain.

"That was stupid, then," Marcus said (which I couldn't really argue with).

Mr Fullerman gave us some instructions. **"Don't turn over the paper until I tell you to. Then write your name and your class at the top, please."**

He asked us a few other things about **pens,** **paper** and that kind of thing.

Did we have everything we needed for the TEST?

I need the answers,

I whispered to AMY, who sighed.

Mr Fullerman told us, **"CONCENTRATE, everyone."**

So that's what I did.

I CONCENTRATED

... just not on the TEST.

I wrote my name carefully and answered the first question. (All good so far.)

But after the SECOND question, my PEN suddenly STOPPED working, which was annoying.

I turned my paper over and SCRIBBLED really HARD to try and get the pen working again. Then I tried SHAKING the pen when Mr Fullerman wasn't looking. I could have asked him for a NEW one but he'd made a really BIG point of saying,

> **Does everyone have a pen that WORKS?**
> **Please check NOW because I don't want to be**
> **handing out pens once you've started.**

I said, "YES, SIR," because my pen WAS working THEN.

I looked round 👀 to see if anyone else had a SPARE pen. 👀 Marcus 😊 wouldn't lend me a pen even if he DID have one. I glanced over to AMY'S desk and she HAD a pen. 🙂

So I tried to attract her attention by SCRiBBLing some more to PROVE that my pen had run out.

"It's stopped working," I whispered 🙂 just as the pen started to WORK.

AMY sighed and carried on with her TEST.

I answered the next question, then my pen stopped writing AGAIN. This time I waved it around, which made iNK BLObs come out.

My TEST paper was starting to look a bit MESSY.

All my frantic scribbling and pen-shaking was starting to ANNOY AMY.

She finally pushed her spare pen in my direction.

Here, take it, she said.

I drew a smiley face to say thank you. ☺
Now I had a pen that worked, I could start
answering the rest of the questions. There was
INK on my hand as well, which made a few
splodges on the paper. So I wrote,

— LOOK IT'S A FACE!

(This was an accident - sorry.)

I was ABOUT to get back to the TEST when my
FOOT began to ⋛ **ITCH** ⋛ like it was on
FIRE! Maybe there was something
inside my 🧦 sock BITING me. ➡
I couldn't concentrate.

I tried REALLY HARD to ignore my ITCHY FOOT.
But that didn't work. ALL I could think about was,

ITCHY FOOT ITCHY FOOT ITCHY FOOT
WHY IS MY FOOT SO ITCHY?
AGHHHHHHHHHHHHHHH!

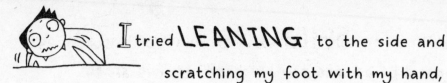

I tried **LEANING** to the side and scratching my foot with my hand, but I couldn't quite reach it. So I grabbed my pen and tried to push it inside my sock. Then I decided the only thing to do was to take OFF my shoe <u>and</u> sock and have a

PROPER scratch.

After a few blissful moments of scratching, it felt **SO MUCH** better that I SIGHED quite loudly. sigghhhhhhhhh

And when I looked up, **AMY** was watching me. She shook her head and carried on doing the TEST.

Scratch

Scratch

(I FORGOT I was using HER pen to scratch with.)

All the pen-SHAKING and FOOT-scratching had taken up a lot more TEST time than I thought. As I was trying to put my sock on, Marcus Meldrew started doing "your foot smells" signs at me.

Then Mr Fullerman told Marcus to

GET ON with the test.

I managed to slip my sock into my pocket so Mr Fullerman didn't SPOT what I'd been doing.

When I FINALLY got back to the TEST some of the questions were really quite HARD. Glancing over in AMY'S direction didn't help much as she was already on a different page.

THEN Mr Fullerman suddenly announced,

You have ten minutes to CHECK your answers carefully.

CHECK them - I hadn't even started most of them.

I tried NOT to WORRY because when I'm in MATHS, ten minutes goes REALLY s l o w l y.

 I thought I had **AGES**.

But THESE ten minutes *whizzed* past and before I could get to the end of the paper, Mr Fullerman was already saying,

"OK, everyone, put down your pens and turn your paper over."

 "NOW?" I said.

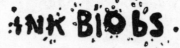 **YES, Tom.**

 I turned over my paper, which was covered in my scribbles, doodles, drawings and

INK BLOBS.

If it was a DOODLE TEST, I'd be right at the

 **TOP** of the class for sure.

"That TEST was EASY, wasn't it?"

Marcus said to me afterwards.

"Sort of," I said.

Then Marcus KEPT bragging. "It's the EASIEST
TEST I've EVER done in my whole entire life.
It was SO EASY that even your stinky feet
didn't put me off," he told me while doing
wafty hand signs at me again.

"I had an ITCHY foot."

Which reminded me that I still had AMY'S pen.
I tried to give it back to her but she said,
"Keep it. You might need to
scratch your other foot as well."

As we left the classroom Marcus was STILL saying
stuff like, "I'll probably get TOP marks!"
I didn't say anything because I had a sneaky feeling
that I hadn't done quite so well in the TEST.

WHAT HAPPENED AFTER the TEST

Mum and Dad had been pretty relaxed about my TEST - right up until I got the letter home saying it might be useful for me to go to the SPECIAL **catch-up classes.** They started asking (QUESTIONS) about how I was doing in school, AND they wrote a note to Mr Fullerman in my school planner.

Normally I don't bother them with my planner, ESPECIALLY as they've been so busy with work. It's easier to write my own comments:

Parents' Comments

Tom is a VERY good boy all the time.

But all of a sudden, Mum and Dad wrote this:

Mr Fullerman,

How is Tom doing in class?
Should we be worried about his progress?
Is there anything more we could do to HELP him?

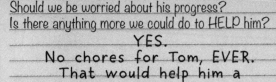

Should we be worried about his progress?
Is there anything more we could do to HELP him?
YES.
No chores for Tom, EVER.
That would help him a
LOT.

I REALLY

wanted to write

next to THAT comment:

(I didn't ... which was hard.) ☹

Mum and Dad were EVEN talking about coming

to SEE Mr Fullerman about ME. I told them there

were LOADS of other kids doing **catch-up class** so

they really didn't have to.

"I'm NOT the only one – honestly."

In the end they decided to wait until parents'

evening, which Mum said was coming up soon.

 (PHEW!)

I was GLAD about THAT because my parents can

be embarrassing when they come near my school.

I was looking forward to Derek's sleepover EVEN
MORE now. BUT when I
reminded Mum about it she told me,

> The sleepover will have to wait. Sorry, Tom.

> WHY?   I wanted to know.

> Because Derek has **catch-up class** as well.
> So no sleepovers until the TEST is over - OK?

Mum was doing her "DON'T ARGUE WITH ME" voice
and wasn't going to change her mind.
I was REALLY fed up and I knew
Derek would be too.

        I went up to my room where I could see
Derek from my window. He was busy writing a
MESSAGE. (We do that sometimes.)
He held up this sign, and didn't look very happy either.

                        So I wrote him another message

to try and make him laugh...

CHIPS →

(Derek laughs.)

I was hoping that **catch-up class** MIGHT even be

☆FUN☆.

(Well ... if not FUN, not as bad as it could be.)

The CATCH-UP CLASS

The **catch-up classes** were being held after school in the library and in our classroom too.

Mr Fullerman said, **"ANYONE can come along if they want a bit of extra help with the test. BUT if you have a letter, I'll see you here."**

That was me then.

"**Put your hand up if you'd like to come along to catch-up class?"**

No one put up their hand. <u>UNTIL</u>

Mr Fullerman mentioned there would be drinks and snacks BEFORE the class to keep us all going.

More kids were KEEN then...

"You can't come just for the drinks and snacks," he added.

(Not so keen then.)

The rest of the day I had to listen to Marcus telling me how well he'd done in his TEST.

Did I tell you how well I did in the TEST?

"You did – LOTS of times," I yawned.
The END of the school day couldn't come fast enough. At LEAST there would be drinks and snacks to look forward to at the **catch-up class.** That was SOMETHING.

HELP yourselves

When the bell went for the end of school most of my class got up to leave and Mr Fullerman (FINALLY) brought out the

SNACKS YES!

"Help yourselves to plain biscuits and WATER!" he said.

(Oh...)

If Mr Fullerman wants to get more kids to stay for **catch-up class,** he'd better UP the snack level (which wouldn't be hard).

I still ate one though. It was better than nothing.

While Mr Fullerman began explaining WHAT we'd all be doing, I started to feel a bit sleepy. I was wondering what Derek was doing in the library and imagining he was having more *FUN* than ME. Then I rested my head on my desk ... just for a minute...

AND THAT'S WHEN
Mr Fullerman WOKE me
UP from the AMAZING
DREAM I was having ABOUT
being TOP of the CLASS,
getting voted on to the
SCHOOL COUNCIL and DUDE3
playing at the school.

(Me awake NOW.)

SO here I am
trying really hard to keep my eyes open while STILL
wondering if Derek is having more FUN than I
am in his **catch-up class** in the library...

A catch-up class quiz... Brilliant!

If I was in the library I wouldn't have fallen asleep because I'd be able to hang out with Derek. I REALLY want to SWAP CLASSES, but I'm not sure HOW. I BET Mr Fullerman won't let me go to the library - especially after I fell asleep.

I'll have to come up with a VERY convincing PLAN, which could be tricky ... hmmmm.

As I'm thinking about what to do, Leroy Lewis puts up his hand and says,

"Can I go and use the study books in the library please, Mr Fullerman?"

(Hah! Like THAT'S going to work!)

Mr Fullerman only goes and says, **"OK, Leroy – they do have more study books there. I'll write you a NOTE to give to Ms Lucas."**

I wasn't expecting THAT to happen.

I watch Leroy take his note and go off
to the library. Then I WAIT a few minutes before
putting <u>MY</u> hand UP and asking the same
QUESTION. I try hard to sound like I really want
to use those STUDY BOOKS and not just
hang out with my best mate (like I do).

 Then Mr Fullerman says,
"If I let you go, Tom, what will
you have to work on?"
And I say the first thing that POPS into my
head, which is,

"STAYING AWAKE?"

"Anything ELSE?"

"Errrr... Reading the study books carefully
and doing the TEST questions without
all the doodles."

(It's a good answer. I think.)

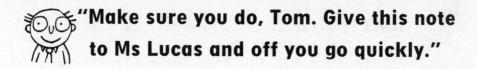 **"Make sure you do, Tom. Give this note to Ms Lucas and off you go quickly."**

I get a bit OVEREXCITED because I can't BELIEVE he's letting me G⊙!

"YES!
THANK YOU, SIR - THAT'S
BRILLIANT!" I SHOUT.

Air punch

Then, in case Mr Fullerman gets suspicious, I add, in a more sensible, less shouty voice, "This will help me a lot, Mr Fullerman."

I don't want him to think I might be trying to **ESCAPE** from the class (which might seem CRAZY but that's EXACTLY what Buster Jones tried to do last week).

Buster Jones is older than me and in the year above. He's one of those kids who seems to get into trouble a **LOT** for doing STUPID things (like lying on the floor when he's not supposed to).

Get off the floor, Buster.

"It's comfy, miss..."

When **Buster** was in DETENTION, he decided to try and **ESCAPE** through the classroom window. (He was on the ground floor - even **Buster**'s not **THAT** DAFT.)
Only, he got **STUCK** - properly wedged in.
Some kids gathered around and just STARED at him.

Derek and I watched what was going on from a safe distance.
Buster started to get really cross that he couldn't get out.

> Don't just STAND there LOOKING at ME. HELP ME OUT!

So a few of them got hold of his leg and started to try and PULL him out. But THAT didn't work. **Buster** tried *wiggling* from side to side but he didn't BUDGE at all. When the teacher (Mr Sprocket) caught him trying to escape detention, he tried to pull **Buster** BACK into the classroom.

It was like a **TUG** of war. **Buster** wasn't happy.

Mr Keen saw what was going on from his office window, and he wasn't happy either.

> What's going on down there?

Eventually Caretaker Stan had to be called to help free Buster from the window. He was in HEAPS of trouble after that.

Detention, Buster.

Mr Keen made a special announcement over the tannoy telling the whole school that no one should EVER try and climb out of a window as it was very dangerous and they were likely to get STUCK.

So I won't be doing anything like THAT. Before Mr Fullerman changes his mind, I gather up my stuff. I'm feeling quite pleased :) with myself because:

1. I'm off to the library. YEAH!

2. I can hang out with Derek. Yeah!

3. I might actually do better in my TEST. YEAH!

4. Derek and I can sit together. Yeah!

5. I don't have to pretend to like the snacks. Yuck.

Brad Galloway puts up his hand and asks if he can go to the library too.

"Why do you need to go, Brad?"

Mr **F**ullerman asks.

 "Because Tom's going," Brad says, which turns out to be the WRONG ANSWER.

I mouth (Sorry, Brad,) to him as I close the door and leave.

As I'm on my way to the library, I hear a DOOR open REALLY **LOUDLY**, followed by VERY STOMPY footsteps coming up the stairs towards me.

I don't really want to EXPLAIN to another teacher what I'm doing. If it's **M**r **K**een he'll keep me chatting for **AGES**.

 Where are you going, Tom?

So I make the QUICK decision to hop into the cloakroom near the library and ...

... HIDE until whoever it is has gone past.

I can just about see out and I realize that it's NOT a teacher, it's BUSTER JONES, who looks like he's in a bit of a hurry.

As he walks past me I breathe a sigh of RELIEF. PHEW. That was close. I'm about to sneak out when Buster comes BACK! He STOPS in front of the glass cabinet where all the photos of the teachers are. I hold my breath and DON'T MOVE. Buster is doing something, but I can't quite see what it is. He's LAUGHING to himself for what seems like AGES. He's very busy. When he finally leaves, and I'm sure he's not coming back ...

OAKFIELD SCHO

I creep out of the cloakroom and take a
 at what **Buster's** been up to.

OH!

He's going to be in SO much trouble if anyone finds
out what he's done.

Whooaah...

Buster's drawn ALL OVER the glass cabinet! While I'm staring  at Buster's handiwork, Ms Lucas opens the library door and calls my name.

Tom Gates!

Which makes me JUMP!

"Aren't you supposed to be in **catch-up class** now? Come along, don't stand around!"

I don't want her to see what Buster's done in case she thinks it was ME who did it.
So I quickly say,
"YES, miss...
I'm coming to the library RIGHT NOW."
(Buster Jones has NO idea what a lucky escape he's just had from a TON more detentions!)

Ms Lucas turns around and I follow her into the library. The first person I see is DEREK, who looks up and waves.

Ms Lucas (who's new in the school) is here to make sure we all do our work. I hand over my note and say, "Mr Fullerman says I can use the study books here to help with my TEST."
Ms Lucas read my note and says,

"OK, Tom. Find a seat."

I head straight towards Derek when she adds,

"Not there, Tom. This note says you and

Derek CHAT too much."

(Thanks a LOT, Mr Fullerman.)

I sit as near to Derek as I can because I REALLY

want to tell him what Buster Jones did to

the TEACHERS' PHOTOS! (Ha!)

Ms Lucas hands me the

study book and some

EXTRA paper.

"You know what you have to

do, don't you, Tom?"

"Yes, Ms Lucas," I say.

The first thing I TRY and do is to tell Derek what

happened. But he can't hear me. What?

So I write him a NOTE, which makes it look

like I'm WORKING HARD when I'm really doing a

drawing of Buster's graffiti.

I finish my note and then give it to the kid in front of me so he can pass it to Derek. →

"Psst! Psst!" I whisper.

"Pass this on to Derek over there." The boy takes the note ...

... OPENS IT UP AND READS IT!

Hey Derek!

Guess what I saw

Buster Jones do? →

He DREW graffiti all over the photos of the teachers in the glass cabinet!

It's very funny.

From Tom ☺

"IT'S NOT FOR YOU!" I hiss. "Pass it to Derek!"

But it's too late.

"Did Buster really do THAT?!"

"Do what?" another kid asks.

"Just PASS it on!" I tell him.

He does — but not to Derek.

My note goes around practically the WHOLE library→ and EVERY KID has a look BEFORE Derek finally gets it.

He mouths "Really?" at me.

Then he writes something on my NOTE and tries to throw it back. Only the note lands on the table next to mine.

Ms Lucas looks up to see what's going on.

"No messing around," she says.

We all pretend to be BUSY.

(I'll pick the note up later.)

For the next TEN minutes I manage to get some work done, while keeping an EYE on the note.

I'm thinking of just sneaking over to pick it up, when in walks Mr Keen with Buster Jones by his side.

Mr Keen says, "I'm sorry to interrupt, Ms Lucas. Buster needs to finish his detention in here, if you wouldn't mind. There's been an incident of graffiti, which Caretaker Stan has asked me to investigate."

Buster is looking down and sort of smiling.

Mr Keen tells Buster,

"Sit OVER THERE and NO talking. You're here to finish off your work quietly. OK, Buster?"

Buster mumbles, "Yes, sir."

"OVER THERE" turns out to be ...

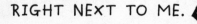

RIGHT NEXT TO ME.

Oh –

Buster gets out his work while I keep my head down and STARE at my book. When I think it's safe, I look up. Buster is STARING at me, and NOT in a good way. He LEANS over and tries to TALK to me.

"Psssssst! Psssssstttt! Gatesy, Gatesy!"

I don't say a word but inside my head I'm thinking, GATESY? THAT'S NOT MY NAME! (Buster likes to give everyone nicknames.)

I keep looking down.

Then he says it AGAIN. "GATESY, you're good at drawing. How do I do this graph thing?"

 He's holding up his work and wants me to HELP him.

(Why ME? I'm not sure what to do now.)

Ms Lucas spots **Buster** bothering me and says, "Buster, leave Tom alone and concentrate on your OWN work."

Which is a RELIEF.

Then **Buster** says quietly,

Yes, MS *MUCUS*.

Ms **L**ucas doesn't notice he's called her the wrong name (he'd get another detention if she did). **Buster** flicks through his book and then *LEANS* over to me AGAIN!

"Did you hear THAT, Gatesy? I said 'MS Mucus'. Ha! I've got nicknames for ALL the teachers."

 I still keep quiet. **Buster** doesn't know that SOME kids have a nickname for HIM too. They call him **"BULLY BUSTER"**. But not to his face, obviously.

"Pssssstt! Pssssstt! GATESEY. Do you want to hear my nicknames for the teachers then?"

I DO — but I don't want to get into trouble, so I don't say anything.

Then he starts telling me anyway.

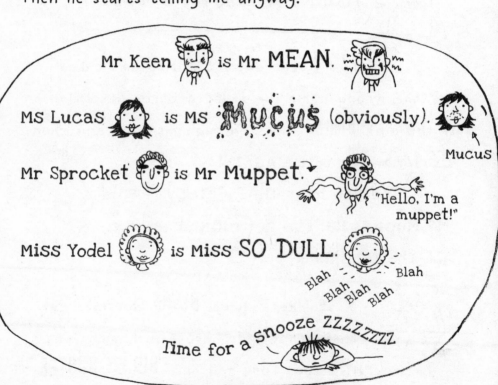

Mr Keen is Mr MEAN.

MS Lucas is MS MUCUS (obviously).

Mucus

Mr Sprocket is Mr Muppet.

"Hello, I'm a muppet!"

Miss Yodel is Miss SO DULL.

Blah Blah Blah Blah Blah

Time for a snooze ZZZZZZZ

I'm trying HARD NOT to LAUGH... but I can't help it! Some of his names are FUNNY.

Buster sees I'm giggling, so he KNOWS I'm listening to what he's saying. Then he adds, "Your teacher, Mr Fullerman, I've got a REALLY good nickname for HIM. Shall I tell you what it is?"

(YES! YES! I REALLY want to know!) I smile a bit but don't say anything out LOUD.

Buster leans even closer to me and says...

It's ...

(Very long pause...)

Mr FULLERBUM.

I do such a LOUD laugh
HA! that even Buster's surprised.

Ms Lucas comes over and tells
ME to move to the END of the table and leave
Buster alone, as if I'm the troublemaker.
Derek is looking over and wondering WHY I'm
LAUGHING. I SO want to tell him what Buster
just said to me. He'll think it's funny, too.

Ha! Mr Fullerbum! I can't wait
until we go home
so I can tell Derek. Then I decide – WHY WAIT?
I'll write another note with a DRAWING on it
and I'll THROW it to him this time.

(Good plan.)

As I start drawing my hand keeps Wobbling because I'm LAUGHING again.

(I'm trying NOT to but it isn't easy.)

Derek This is why I was LAUGHING.

HOW FUNNY IS THIS NICKNAME

for Mr Fullerman?

(Wait for it...)

I'm SO engrossed in my drawing that I don't realize Mr Fullerman has walked into the library. He says something to Ms Lucas which makes me look up. Uh-oh... I just about manage to cover my drawing with my hand. Then I look around and GRAB a BIG book that's next to me and slip my (hilarious) drawing between the pages so he can't SEE IT. Which is a stroke of GENIUS as Mr Fullerman is suddenly STANDING behind me.

THE BIG BOOK OF BIRDWATCHING

Tom, have you finished all of your work?

"I have," I say, hoping he doesn't SPOT my drawing.

Mr Fullerman tells me to gather everything up and come back to class before going home. So that's what I do, but I have a **STRANGE** feeling that I'm being STARED at. I glance over to Buster. He's FOUND the note Derek threw at me, and from the look on his FACE, he's read it.

Buster doesn't look happy.

I have to walk past him to leave the library and he says to me, "OI, GATESY! You and your mate Derek need to KEEP THIS to yourselves, RIGHT?" He's waving the note.

I kind of nod as I *SQUEEZE* past him to make a *BREAK* for freedom (back to my class).

I can't WAIT to go home now. I'm in a BIG
hurry to meet Derek at the school gate.
When he turns up, the first thing we have
to do is HIDE from Buster.

I tell Derek EVERYTHING that happened.

 "Buster READ the NOTE about his graffiti."

"Oh no..."

 "Buster told me WE have to keep quiet.
He doesn't KNOW the WHOLE library
read the note."

"ALL those kids."

(I save the BEST until last.)

"Buster has nicknames for the teachers and
guess what he CALLS Mr Fullerman..."

"Tell me."

 **"Mr FULLERBUM!"**

Derek is in stitches.  Ha! Ha!

We both are. Ha! Ha! Ha!

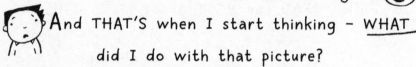 "I drew a PICTURE of him to send you – it's REALLY **FUNNY!**"

"Let's see it then," Derek says.

And THAT'S when I start thinking – WHAT did I do with that picture?

I have a **HORRIBLE** feeling that I might have left it in one of the library books.

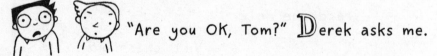 "Are you OK, Tom?" Derek asks me.

"I'm not sure – I can't remember WHAT I did with THAT picture. I could be in a lot of trouble if someone finds it!"

"WHY?"

"A TEACHER could find it," I explain.

"They won't know YOU drew it though. It's not like you wrote your NAME on it or anything."

Hmmmmm...

(Let me think about that.)

"Did I sign it?"

"You didn't sign it, did you, Tom?" Derek asks me.

(Still thinking...)

"Why would I sign it? That's a CRAZY thing to do," I tell him.

"You signed the drawing, didn't you?"

"Maybe... I HAVE to find it before anyone else does - for lots of reasons. It won't help my chances of being voted on to the school council. I think I wrote that TESTS were annoying too," I explain to Derek.

"And I drew Mrs Worthingtash."

(I REALLY need my drawing.)

All the way back home I keep thinking ... WHAT if someone finds MY DRAWING?

Derek is doing his BEST to make me feel like everything will be fine. But it's not really working.

"What's the WORST thing that can happen?" he asks me.

"I can think of LOADS of bad things that could happen," I tell him.

TOM GATES, what do you say about THIS?

"Actually, so can I."

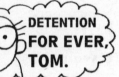

DETENTION FOR EVER, TOM.

"LIKE what?" I want to know.

"Well, imagine if Ms Lucas finds the drawing. She could pass it on to

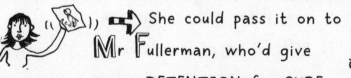

Mr Fullerman, who'd give you a DETENTION for SURE.

If Mr Fullerman was in a **BAD** mood, he might send you to see Mr Keen."

"Do you think so?"

"He might do. Then, Mr Keen could write a letter home to your mum and dad."

"NOT another letter," I sigh.

Before Derek goes into his house, he ADDS,

"UNLESS..."

"Unless WHAT?" I want to know.

"UNLESS **Bully Buster** finds the drawing. Remember, he was in the library too."

(How could I forget?) Gatesy. Gatesy.

"**Buster** might use your drawing to get himself OUT of trouble. You know what he's like."

No, Sir, I don't know who did the graffiti. BUT TOM GATES did THIS drawing.

(I didn't think about that.)

"But **THAT'S** not going to happen. It will probably get lost and no one will find it, so don't WORRY about it, TOM."

Then Derek goes into his house. Bye!

Everyone keeps telling me not to worry about things.

Finding a half-eaten wafer at the bottom of my bag helps ...

... a little.

First thing tomorrow morning, I'm going BACK to the library to find the *book* I hid my drawing in. Though I'm not totally sure which one it was.

In my  HEAD I'm thinking of a PLAN that will solve my very tricky problem.

Also (in my head), I'm thinking how much easier EVERYTHING would be if only I had just one

(or maybe two)

SUPERPOWERS.

HERE ARE MY TOP FIVE SUPERPOWERS

1. SUPER SPEEDY

I could zoom back to school and whizzzzz around the library until I find my drawing. THEN I'd zzzzipppp back home and be the first one at dinner.

2. SUPER (invisible)

An EXCELLENT POWER for avoiding Mum and Dad when they want me to tidy stuff.

Where's Tom gone?

Also GOOD for avoiding Delia,

Tom

Bully Buster AND **Mr Fullerman**

if he finds my drawing.

Where's Tom?

Tom Gates, did you draw this?

3. SUPER SMART

 "Ask me ANYTHING."

No more **catch-up classes** for me because I'd know the answers to EVERYTHING.

Delia couldn't argue with me and Marcus would have to stop BRAGGING about how brilliant he is at TESTS.

"I'm good at TESTS." "So am I..."

4. SUPER FLYER (Who doesn't want to fly?)

 "BYE."

5. SUPERHUMAN MEMORY

(This would be so useful.)

With this superpower I'd HAVE:

* Remembered ALL the answers to the TEST.

* Been at the TOP of the class.

* NOT been in **catch-up class.**

* NOT done that drawing of Mr Fullerbum.

* NOT forgotten to take that drawing with me.

 Memory In • Out

(Sadly, I don't have that superpower.)

I was SO busy eating my (old) wafer, I completely
forgot that Mum is working late tonight. Mum and
Dad have both been really busy lately. Especially Dad,
who's spending LOADS more time in his shed.
(I think that's where he is now. 🏠) Mum's left
one of her notes on the fridge. I have a read as it's
for all of us.

HI FAMILY!
   I'm working late tonight (in case you've
forgotten).
   TOM – I hope catch-up class went well (don't
worry about the test).
   FRANK – As you're busy too, I've asked
Granny Mavis to make dinner.
   ONLY KIDDING! Ha!
   I've made it already. It's in the fridge.
DELIA – Could you be IN CHARGE of heating up
the dinner and dishing it out, please? That would
be very helpful.
   See you later! No arguing PLEASE.
                              Love Mum xx

As I read Mum's note ONE bit makes me GROAN out loud. Delia - could you be IN CHARGE?

(Why?)

Delia already thinks she's the BOSS. Do as I SAY.

When Mum and Dad aren't around, she's always trying to tell me what to do.

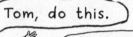 Tom, do this.

Tom, do that!

(She's done it before.)

Just in case dinner goes horribly WRONG Sigh...

(getting burnt, that kind of thing),

I decide to 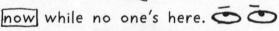 GRAB a SNACK

now while no one's here. ⊙ ⊙

I SPOT a LARGE bag of crisps on a high shelf.

Then I SEE what flavour they are.

SEAWEED & WOOD FLAVOUR CRISPS

YUCK!  I'm not that desperate YET.

I settle on a carton of drink,  a banana
and a packet of cheesy crackers. → Cheesy Crackers Yum!
I put (HIDE) everything in my bag,
then go to say "HI!" to Dad who's out in
his shed on the phone. I wave "⚡" and he waves
back. Then I RUB my stomach and do my
"I'm REALLY hungry and I KNOW you have
a biscuit tin" face. Which WORKS.
Dad points to the tin and
nods his head while he carries on talking.

THE GOOD NEWS

for me is that there
are two VERY NICE-looking
cookies inside. There are a few fig rolls too,
but I'm not touching those.

LARGE

Small

FIG ROLLS

(If there was NOTHING else
around, I might eat one.
But I'm in LUCK today
with the cookies.)

I take a **bite** out of the $\mathbb{BIG}$ one  then wave again at Dad as I leave.

Dad looks SURPRISED when he sees me eating the

$\mathring{\mathbb{I}}\mathbb{BIG}$ cookie, like he'd forgotten it was there.

(He had.)

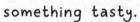 I whisper, "There are still some fig rolls left,"

as I close the door behind me – quickly.

As I walk back to the kitchen, Rooster is

jumping up and down on the other side of the

garden fence like he KNOWS I'm eating

something tasty.

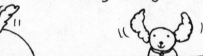

NO WAY, Rooster! ~YUM

I tell him as I head into the kitchen.

Delia's come downstairs and she's reading Mum's note.

> I have to do everything around here.
> It's **NOT FAIR!**

she says in a really grumpy voice. Straight away, I put the cookie in my bag so she can't see it and PINCH it from me. (That's happened before.) Even with her sunglasses on, I can tell Delia's giving me a **LOOK**.

HEY!

> If you want dinner you'll have to eat it NOW.
> **I'M** going **OUT**.

"It's a bit early for dinner," I point out.

> **Tough** – it's NOW or NEVER, and Mum said you're **NOT** allowed to eat anything on the CLEAN sofa. **OR ELSE**.

"I'll eat dinner now then." (Like I have a choice.)

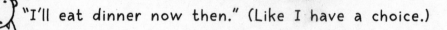

I bet Mum <u>didn't</u> say "OR ELSE". That's just
Delia being all bossy and thinking she's in charge.

Delia waves me away with her hand, saying,
"It's not ready YET. You don't need to
be here." Which suits me FINE. I can
finish off my cookie and watch some
TV without her bothering ME. ☺

Shoo Shoo

It also takes my mind OFF the Mr FB drawing
I LEFT in the library. (That's what I'm calling
it from now on.) I might get a BRAINWAVE and
SUDDENLY remember exactly which book I
left it in ... with my

Brainwave

SUPER HUMAN
→ MEMORY ←

(If only.)

I head off to the living room, then I make some room on the sofa to S P R E A D myself out by chucking the scatter cushions on the floor.

Once I'm comfy I start watching cartoons while eating my COOKIE. Every time I "LAUGH," crumbs go flying all over the place. I use my hand to sweep them into

a neat pile, then I carefully push them on to the floor.

I'm still enjoying my cookie when I THINK I can

hear Delia coming to get me.

So I SHOVE what's left of

it UNDER my leg,

which SEEMS like a

sensible thing to do.

Hidden cookie

I'm WAITING for her to come in.
But there's no sign of her so far... Nope, it's
a false alarm. So I take out my cookie and
that's when I spot a PROBLEM.
Some of the choc chips have

MELTED

on to my leg AND ON THE SOFA as well. (The SOFA
that I'm not supposed to EAT on – OR ELSE.)

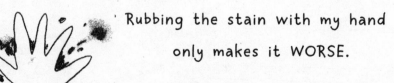

Rubbing the stain with my hand
only makes it WORSE.

AND much BIGGER too.

It's almost the same size as one of the scatter cushions now. Which gives me an IDEA! I *LEAN* over the sofa to find one of the cushions and then carefully place it over the stain,

WHICH

WORKS A

TREAT!

You can't see a thing any more. But then I spot another problem exactly where I was kneeling. It's ANOTHER stain! (Oh, great.) I grab a different cushion and cover that one too. NOW seems like a good time to go into the kitchen, even if dinner isn't ready yet.

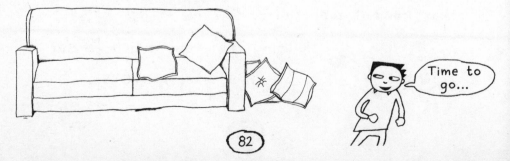

Time to go...

Delia is as pleased to see me as ever.

"Your dinner's over there. I'm
FAR too nice to you,"
she says, pointing to my food.

"You're not THAT nice," I tell her.

"I made you PIE, how much nicer could I be?"
Delia tries to convince me.

"What's in the pie?
It might be something I don't like."

"Just eat it, Mr Fussy," Delia tells me sternly.
"I need you to do something USEFUL for
a change and tell Mum and Dad that I'm at a
FRIEND'S house but I won't be back LATE. OK?
WHAT ARE YOU GOING TO TELL THEM?"

"You've got <u>NO</u> friends and you're going
to be really LATE," I tell her. (Ha! Ha!)

 "Very FUNNY, Tom."

"Thank you," I say, and I ask her  what's in the pie again. Delia doesn't answer. (She's ignoring me.)

As I'm getting hungry, I eat some anyway ... and  It's DELICIOUS!

"Do you like it then, Tom?" Delia says before she leaves.

"Mmmmm... What kind of pie is it?" I ask her again with my mouth full.

"Didn't I tell you? Just slug and crunchy frog. ENJOY!"

I know Delia's joking - but it just doesn't taste the same now.

(**I** still eat it though.) The green
beans I spread around the plate so it looks like I've
had most of them.

There's a real SKILL to hiding food you don't
like. I do it at school and at Granny Mavis's house.

Lumpy mince hidden under my cutlery

Tuna and mushrooms hidden under mashed potato

It's especially useful if you don't like TUNA. That
fish is always popping up where you LEAST expect it.

Tuna burger

Tuna hiding in pasta

Tuna on potato wedges

(WRONG)

As I've finished my dinner (sort of) I head upstairs to
my room. I can still see **D**erek from my window, which
reminds me about my lost Mr FB drawing. I wonder if
Derek can remember <u>what</u> book I left it in? (I can't.)

I write out a SIGN and put it up at my window
to ask Derek, who looks confused.

I have a FEELING that the book had BIRDS on it,
so I do another sign. I draw the book on one side
and Mr Fullerbum on the other.

Which makes Derek laugh, and I start laughing too!
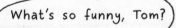

I don't notice Dad is in the room until he says,

What's so funny, Tom?

He's finished work and has
come upstairs to see me.

I'm holding my Mr FB drawing tightly so Dad can't see it. "Nothing – it's just Derek being funny," I tell Dad.

"A birdwatching book? Are you interested in BIRDWATCHING then?" Dad must have read my sign, so I say,

"YES I am – very interested. I'm taking this book out of the library tomorrow."

"Your Uncle Kevin and I used to go out birdwatching when we were kids. KEVIN had all the right GEAR to wear. You can imagine," Dad laughs.

(I can.)

"How about we read a story together once I've had dinner?"

I nod enthusiastically. "Speaking of dinner, I'm surprised you had room for yours after EATING my BIG cookie."

(Oops.)

"I left LOADS of fig rolls and a cookie for you."

"The small one. YES, I saw that."

"I was very hungry - AND Delia told me that dinner was slug and crunchy frog PIE. It almost put me off," I point out.

Dad LAUGHS and says, "That sounds like something Granny Mavis would make! I hope you left some for me?"

"Loads."

I'm still holding on to my drawing when Dad goes downstairs to eat. While I'm waiting for him to come and read stories, I brush my teeth, get ready for bed and then think about which book would be good to choose.

I pick out a few ... and wait.

and wait...

When I can't wait any longer, I go
downstairs to see where he is.

Mum's just come back from work and
is surprised to see me.

> Are you still up? I thought you'd
> be in bed by now.

Then Mum gives me a hug and asks
about **catch-up class.**

"It was OK. But then Delia said dinner was
and crunchy frog pie."

"Is Delia here?" Mum wants to know.
(This is where I'm supposed to say that Delia's
at her FRIEND'S and won't be late. Instead I say
something that sounds a bit similar.)

> Delia's gone out
> to buy ...
> a pet.

89

"A PET. Are you SURE? That's ALL I need."

I just say, "Mmmmmmm," because Mum

looks a bit CROSS and I was only joking.

"Where's your dad – in the shed?" she asks.

"I came down to find him. He said we'd read a

story before bed."

"Sorry, Tom. Let's go and see where he's

got to."

Dad's not in the kitchen or the shed.

As we go back to the kitchen Mum says,

"Well he's EATEN, I can see that."

Empty plate

Then we head to the front room – and there's Dad

lying on the sofa.

"BRILLIANT,"

Mum says.

(But not in a good way.)

90

SCHOOL COUNCIL

ELECTIONS

Do you want to become a school councillor?

WELL NOW'S YOUR CHANCE!

The school council makes lots of important
decisions about what goes on in Oakfield School.
Design a POSTER that tells your classmates
why they should vote for

YOU!

Good luck, everyone.
The countdown begins NOW!

This is a **BIG** moment for me. I've been voted on to the SCHOOL COUNCIL, and I'm about to make a **SPEECH** in front of the **WHOLE** school. **AMY** is clapping and everyone is "CHEERING".

HOORAY!

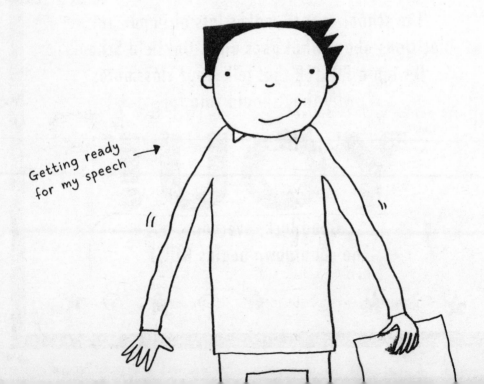

Getting ready for my speech →

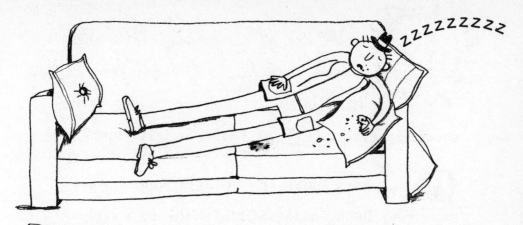

Dad's fast asleep with the TV on, and he's clutching a half-eaten, slightly melted choc-chip cookie.

 "NOW you can see WHY I don't like ANYONE eating on the sofa, Tom. LOOK at those CHOCOLATE STAINS under his leg!"

(I'd forgotten about those.)

Mum thinks the stains are DAD'S fault. I decide that NOW is a good time to go back to bed – just before Mum wakes Dad up.

(I still have those snacks in my school bag too.)

In the morning We're all having breakfast when Mum says, "Do you know HOW LONG it took me to get those chocolate stains **OUT** of the sofa last night?"

I keep quiet and so does Dad. I was expecting Delia to say SOMETHING to me about the "PET" joke. But Mum must have forgotten about it when she saw the SOFA STAINS. So that's good. Then Mum says, "While I remember, I might have to work this weekend, and your dad's kindly volunteered to HELP me."

"HAVE I?" Dad says, sounding surprised.

"YES, Frank. **AND**, Tom, we really need you to do something for us," Mum adds.

(Uh-oh - whenever Mum says THAT it doesn't always end the way I *hope* it might.)

We really need you to do something for us...

 Tidy your room.

 Be nice to your sister.

 Find Granddad's TEETH.

 So I'm waiting to HEAR what they need me to do.

We REALLY need you to ... go to your COUSINS' during the day.

 (Which is not so bad, but I have a better idea.)

"Can I go to Derek's house instead?"

I can see that Mum is trying to work out a reason to say NO.

Derek's Mum and Dad are very busy, and you can't stay here because Delia's going out.

Delia says, Shame...

 But I'm glad I don't have to stay with her.

"You have fun at the cousins', don't you?"
Dad asks me.

"SOMETIMES," I say, which is true.
"I have MORE fun at Derek's."

"I know what you mean," Dad says, agreeing
with me.

I WISH Granny Mavis and Granddad Bob were
here, then I could go and hang out with them.
But they're on holiday. We've had a postcard
from them already. They look like they're having
a GREAT time.

I hope I have a good time at the cousins'.
(Now that I don't have a
CHOICE about going.)

Dear EVERYONE!

We're having a wonderful time on the ship. Though it took a while to get used to the  WAVES. One was so big, Bob's teeth flew out of his mouth and landed in a lady's dinner. So far we've been swimming, dancing and waterskiing, which was great fun. The postcard is a photo the crew took of us.

To: Family Gates

24 Castle Road

Lots of love,
Bob and Mavis xx

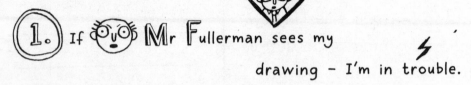

Here are all the REASONS I need to get my (Mr FB) drawing BACK.

1. If Mr Fullerman sees my

    drawing – I'm in trouble.

2. If Ms Lucas finds my

    drawing – I'm in trouble.

3. If Bully Buster finds my

    drawing – he'll get me into trouble.

4. If Mr Keen gets shown my

    drawing – I'll be in trouble.

5. If Mum and Dad are

told about my drawing – I'll be in HUGE trouble.

    (I could go on.)

I have a PLAN.

On my way to school I explain my
PLAN to Derek, who's keen to help.

My PLAN
goes like
THIS:

Go to the library, ➡ find book,
find drawing IN book, YEAH! ➡
take drawing in book BACK, ➡ ☺
show drawing to Derek, HIGH five,
then get rid of drawing for
GOOD. bin

Derek says, It's a GOOD PLAN.

The first person we see in school is Norman, who's

excited to tell us something.

"I have NEW glasses."

(They look exactly the same to me.)

Then Norman tells us he's learning a new instrument

but won't tell us what it is. He says it's a surprise. "I'll

bring it over to band practice and play you my new

tune." (He doesn't know that it's been cancelled.)

"It's cancelled. Sorry, Norman."

"Awwwwwwwwwwwwwwwwwwwwwwwwww."

(He does now.)

Mr Keen is standing by the door and saying
"Hello" as kids walk into school,
while doing a SPOT check on school
uniform too.

No capes ...
or masks...

"Really?"

Then Mr Keen
says to me, "GOOD MORNING, TOM."
But it sounds like he's just said,
"GOOD DRAWING, TOM,"
like he's SEEN my drawing. (He hasn't.)
"Morning, sir," I say, then tell Derek,
"We need to go to the LIBRARY NOW."
"I'll cover for you if Mr Fullerman asks where you
are," Norman says.
"Thanks, Norman." It's a good idea but not part
of the plan.

 I just hope whatever Norman tells
Mr Fullerman will make sense.

Tom's not here because he's been taken away by ALIENS.

BYE!

Caretaker Stan is still cleaning off the pen marks that **Buster** drew on the glass cabinet.

"**Bully Buster** was here,"
I whisper to Derek as we walk past.
Derek says, "Oh, no he's not - he's OVER there."
We manage to avoid **Buster** by hiding behind our bags, then make it to the LIBRARY without being stopped by any teachers (or bumping into **Buster** again).

Don't move

But when we get there it's ...

... CLOSED.  "Oh no!" I sigh.

We press our faces up against

the glass and take a good look through the door.

 "Can you see anything?" Derek asks me.

"Books - lots of books," I say (like that

wasn't obvious already).

Then I SPOT a book that might be the ONE.

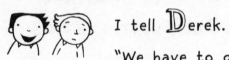

It's THE BIG BOOK OF BIRDWATCHING.

"I think that's the book I put the drawing into,"

 I tell Derek.

"We have to get it RIGHT NOW,"

I say excitedly.

"Right NOW you boys should be in class,"

Mrs Nap says, which makes us both

JUMP!

"YES, Mrs Nap - we're going now."

She watches us leave and I tell Derek,

"We'll HAVE to come back later – maybe lunchtime. I KNOW it's in there."

(PLAN B it is then.)

Luckily I'm not THAT late for class, but I wonder if Norman has made an excuse for me already?

From the way Mr Fullerman is looking at me I'm guessing he might have. **"HURRY UP, TOM. I'm glad to see the GIANT BIRD Norman saw didn't pick you up and take you away for ever."**

Put me down. I'll be late for school.

(Norman made an excuse.)

As I sit down Marcus says, "Hello, GATESY."

HOW does he know that **Bully Buster** was calling me THAT?

"I think it's a catchy nickname – GATESY."

He says it AGAIN.

"That's **NOT** my name, Marcus Meldrew-ey," I say to show him how annoying it is.

"Tom's got a new nickname," Marcus says to **AMY**.

"No I haven't."

"It's GATESY. GATESY, GATESY, GATESY."

Marcus starts singing it.

"It's NOT my new nickname," I tell **AMY** again.

"Whatever. You're BOTH being ANNOYING," she says – which shuts us up.

But not for long...

"I heard that **Buster Jones** has got FUNNY nicknames for ALL the teachers too," Marcus says.

I'm not going to tell Marcus what they are because he'll BLAB them to everyone (even the teachers).

Mr Sprocket, do you know that **Buster** calls you Mr Muppet?

Instead I pick up my pen and start doodling a few nickname ideas of my OWN. (<u>Not</u> for me - for Marcus, who's leaning over my shoulder.)

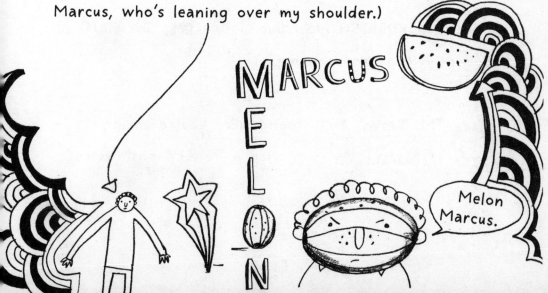

"Hey! That's MY name!" Marcus says.

"Nothing gets past you, Marcus," I say and carry on doodling.

"This could be YOUR new nickname, Marcus."

MARCUS MELDREW

written backwards is ...

WERDLEM SucRAM

He's not impressed.  Hmmph.

"That's a RUBBISH nickname. I like M. Drew. It sounds like a proper name."

"M. Drew? That sounds like you're saying 'ANDREW' but with a REALLY posh voice."

Ha! **AMY LAUGHS** when I say that.

(Marcus doesn't.)

"Lots of famous people use their initials, so <u>I</u> could

be **MM**. I like that," he tells me.

LOADS of ideas flood into my head for what

MM could stand for. So I carry on doodling...

I'm so busy doodling that I don't hear **Mr Fullerman**

call my name until he says out LOUD...

DRAWING AGAIN, TOM?

I put down my pen and look up slowly.

 "Oh ... THIS drawing, sir? I'm just doodling."

You've been doing FAR too much doodling lately, Tom, haven't you?

 GULP (I hope he isn't talking about THAT

drawing.)

I say, "Yes, sir. I have."

Then I wait to see what else he says to

me. ——————————————▶ (Nothing.)

 Phew

PLAN B needs to be put into action as soon as possible because I have to get that drawing back so I can stop worrying about who might find it.

This whole situation is getting trickier and trickier.

3

But first ...
DRAMA

Before I can go back to the library, we have a
DRAMA lesson in the hall. Mr Fullerman takes
us all downstairs and we walk past the library on
the way. IF ONLY I could just ⟹NIP inside

and GRAB the book, then ˋ˙ta-da!˙ˊ Everything

would be sorted!

But the door's still closed so I'm going

to have to WAIT.

Sigh.

← Books

↳ Books

(A superpower would REALLY come in
handy right now, that's for sure.)

Most of the time DRAMA LESSONS are OK.
Some are more fun than others depending on who's
taking the class.
Mr Fullerman always makes us do these weird face
exercises before we start.

(Ooooo...) (Aeeey...) (EEEee...)

Sometimes we have to swing our arms around and
shake our hands. Spinning in a
circle can be tricky if you end up near
Norman or Julia Morton.

I feel
sick...

Once Mrs Nap took us for DRAMA and she
made us pretend to be...

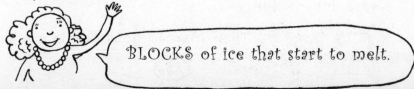

BLOCKS of ice that start to melt.

Some kids REALLY got into it. Especially

Solid who made an EXCELLENT ice cube.

He said it was a very HOT day

and that's why he melted quickly.

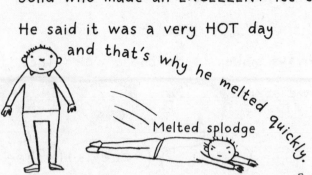

Melted splodge

Melting.

(Indrani)

Today's lesson sounds OK though. Mr Fullerman

wants us to make up a short SCENE from a day in

the life of the school and ACT it out.

"You could choose something REAL or use your imagination to THINK of something that has NEVER happened before in school!"

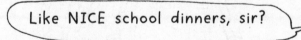

Like NICE school dinners, sir?

Brad Galloway suggests, which makes us all laugh.

I'm thinking that this could be a really good lesson

and a lot of fun...

 Then Marcus gets put in my group.

What?

110

"Hello again, Gatesy!" he says to me, which straight away is annoying.

So I say, "Hello WERDLEM – that's your new nickname!"

Marcus doesn't call me Gatesy again.

AMY, Solid, Florence and Trevor Peters are in our group too. Normally when it comes to deciding what our play is going to be about, we wouldn't get a word in edgeways with Marcus. Listen to me.

But Solid comes up with a BRILLIANT idea that we ALL AGREE on. (Even Marcus does.)

What do you think?

Great!

Yeah, it's OK.

GENIUS!

We're going to act out the time when Buster Jones got STUCK in the window.
Marcus is Mr Keen, who gets cross (he'll be good at that). Solid is Buster, Florence is the teacher and the rest of us are the kids who try to pull Buster out.

Our rehearsal goes pretty well...

I'm pretending to **heave**
Solid through the window
with Trevor.

Solid is doing a
good job of being STUCK.

But when we do the whole scene in front of
the class, Marcus gets carried away pretending to be
Mr Keen and BLURTS out, "RIGHT, Buster –
detention for a WHOLE YEAR."

Everyone laughs. Solid says, "A YEAR?"

"Make it TWO YEARS – because I know it
was YOU who drew all those moustaches
and graffiti on the TEACHERS' photos."

(WHAT? I can't believe he's just said that!)

Marcus has just TOLD the whole class and
Mr Fullerman that **Buster** did the graffiti. We
finish our little school play ... and get a BIG round
of applause.

"What did you say THAT for?"
I whisper to Marcus.

"I'll just say I made it
all up – it's called ACTING." He sounds very sure
of himself.

While we watch the other plays I remind Marcus,
"IF **Buster** gets found out he'll think it
was ME who BLABBED and told everyone."

"You _did_ tell everyone." Marcus looks at me, puzzled.

"No, I didn't – I just drew a picture
on a note for Derek, that's all."

"Adam Bright told me your note got passed
around the WHOLE LIBRARY in **catch-up
class,** so everyone knew it was **Buster.** Then he
went and told me!"

"They just read it – I didn't say they could. Who else have you told?" I ask Marcus.

 "Just a few kids."

"How few?"

"Not many."

(He means EVERYONE.)

I know who did the graffiti – Buster.

It was Buster.

Buster Jones.

Buster Jones.

It was Buster.

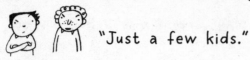 So much for trying to keep things quiet. ("Keep it to yourself," Buster told me and Derek. There's no chance NOW.)

Mr Fullerman CONGRATULATES the whole class for all the EXCELLENT plays we put on. Our group gets a special mention for some...

"Excellent acting! But let's make sure none of you do what Buster tried to do. No escaping from lessons, OK?"

"Yes, sir," we all say.

Walking back to class, I can see the library is now OPEN! (At last.) That's the first place I'm going to go when the bell goes.

There's TEN MINUTES to go before lunch, and Mr Fullerman wants us ALL to have some...

"QUIET and CALM time. Let's all take a moment to RELAX," he says while wafting his arms around.

It's not easy to do when I have so many things on my mind, like TESTS, lost drawings, Buster.

Mr Fullerman suggests that we fill in our reading records, get out our books or even catch up with some other work.

Marcus starts HUMMING, which is annoying and not very RELAXING at all. So to help ZONE Marcus out, I do a doodle instead.

It's amazing how much it helps.

I keep going until the bell goes for lunch. Norman says he'll come with me to the library to help look for...

"You know what."

Straight away, Marcus is being nosy. "What are you looking for?"

"Nothing," we both say. (I'm not telling Marcus, that's for sure.)

In the library Ms Lucas asks us, "Are you looking for something in particular, boys?"

"I'm looking for a BOOK," I say.

"We have a lot of those here," she laughs.

"It's a SPECIAL book - a BIG BOOK," Norman adds.

"Well the BIG reference books are over there, but you better be quick because I have book club starting soon, and they'll all be sitting in THAT section too," she says, pointing to where the BIG books are.

"Right, OK – PLAN B." I say to Norman. Then I head towards my **catch-up class** seat and LOOK around to see if I can SPOT my drawing in any of the books. Norman starts reading – which isn't exactly helpful, but I leave him to it. There are a LOT of BIG books and now I can't remember which one it was.

I start flicking through some of them as the book club kids start to arrive and sit down around me. My drawing's not here.

    But I keep looking carefully ...

... as more and more book club kids sit down around me.

Then I SUDDENLY SPOT

THE BIG BOOK OF BIRDWATCHING.

YES! It MIGHT be that one. I GRAB it and hold on tightly.

"Have you found the right BOOK, Tom?" Ms Lucas asks me. "I need to start book club now if you want to take one OUT."

"This one please, Ms Lucas."

(Norman is still reading.)

"Trust you to pick a reference book that's NOT supposed to be taken out of the library," she tells me.

I can't look for my drawing surrounded by all these book club kids. So I ask Ms Lucas again (and do a sad face).

"OK, Tom – JUST this once. But keep a close eye on it and don't leave it lying around. Take it home with you and then bring it back tomorrow, OK?"

"It won't leave my side," I say.

(Norman is still reading.)

119

Ms Lucas makes a note of which one I'm taking. "Don't forget, Tom – look after this book, won't you?"

I take **THE BIG BOOK OF BIRDWATCHING** and head out of the door. Norman decides to start JUMPING behind me.

("(PLAN B ⟩ is nearly COMPLETE!)

"Did my JUMPING work then?" Norman says.

"Yes," I tell Norman. Because I just want to look through the book and FIND MY Mr FB drawing!

(AT LAST.)

I'm trying to flick through the pages and walk
at the same time, which is not easy to do.
(Norman is still JUMPING.)
We meet up with Solid
and Derek, who asks me,
"Did you find the YOU KNOW WHAT yet?"
I pick up the book and shake it. But
my drawing doesn't fall out.
"OH NO, don't tell me I've got the
wrong BOOK!"
"I was looking forward to seeing your
drawing," Norman says.

"I'm NOT doing another one."
Derek, Norman and Solid look
disappointed for me.

"It's not inside this book, so it MUST still be in
the library," I sigh.

 PLAN C it is then...

(I'm not sure exactly what  is yet.) Norman STARTS jumping again and says, "I've got something GOOD to tell you."

So we all listen carefully.

"Did you know that if you put the word CHICKEN in front of your surname, it sounds like a proper FANCY dinner?"

No we did not.

"Try it!" Norman suggests.

So we do. Some names work better than others...

Chicken Meldrew   Chicken Gates

Chicken Fingle   Chicken Porter

Chicken Stewart   Chicken Galloway

Chicken Lewis   Chicken Keen

Chicken Worthington   Chicken Fullerman

It's the BEST thing I've done all week.

Now I have to LUG **THE BIG BOOK OF BIRDWATCHING** around in class. Other kids are looking at me and probably thinking,

"WHY THE BIG BOOK?"

So I put it on the floor under my table before Marcus turns up. Then I find myself doodling (like you do) on the edge of my desk.

Look! It's two monsters hanging around.

I stop drawing when **Mr Fullerman** says, **"Can you all listen please?"** (Pen down.) **"I don't have to remind you that DRAWING on school property is taken VERY seriously indeed."** (WHOOPS...)

I cover up my monsters FAST and pretend I haven't drawn anything at all.

I think he's talking about the  **graffiti** that **Buster Jones** did.

Technically, I didn't actually SEE **Buster** draw on the glass. I just saw what it looked like AFTER he'd finished. Marcus is sitting next to me now and (for a change) doesn't say anything either.

I really don't want to TELL on **Buster Jones,** THAT'S for sure. I've been trying to AVOID him, which hasn't been easy.

Everywhere I go he seems to be there, kind of GLARING, while I've been hiding.

Which won't be so easy to do now I have this massive BOOK to look after. I could leave it at school now I know my drawing's not inside.

What I really need to do is go back to the library and *SWAP* it for the right book that has my drawing inside. I could get Norman to do some more JUMPING to distract Ms Lucas while I find a different book. As I'm working out PLAN C, Mr Fullerman says, in front of the WHOLE class,

"Tom, Ms Lucas wanted me to remind YOU to take your BIG BOOK OF BIRDWATCHING home with you. Do you have it here?"

"Yes, sir." He waits for me to show him. Now my WHOLE class have seen I have a birdwatching book.

"Are you really interested in birdwatching, Tom?" AMY asks, looking at the book.

I should say "No".

Instead I hear myself say, "Yes I am."

125

"What do you know about birdwatching then?"

she asks.

"LOADS of interesting stuff ... about birds ... and how to watch them."

"That makes you a TWITCHER," AMY LAUGHS.

Which sounds a bit HARSH if you ask me. I smile at first and pretend not to be bothered. Then I say, "You're right - I AM a TWIT for getting such a HEAVY book."

"You're a TWITCHER, Tom. It's someone who watches birds. I'm NOT saying you're a TWIT," AMY explains.

"I AM - YOU'RE A TWIT," Marcus says, joining in.

(That's all I need.)

"Why have you got out a birdwatching book anyway? That's weird," he adds.

"It's a SECRET. I was going to tell you, but you're not great at keeping secrets."
(Marcus HATES not being told secrets.)

"Oh, GO ON - tell me! I won't say anything." "Well ... are you sure you want to know?"

"Yes!"

"I've heard that if you have an unusual HOBBY, it helps you get elected to the school council. The teachers love it."

"Really?"

"It's TRUE!"

Marcus has already made a LIST of reasons to vote for HIM. He thinks I might STEAL it - so he's got his arm over it. (I bet he adds an unusual hobby to his list now.)

This afternoon we're ALL going to be working on our school council election posters. It's turning out to be quite a good day after all (if I don't think about my missing drawing, and quite a few other things too).

Here are TOP FIVE REASONS
TO BE VOTED ON TO THE SCHOOL COUNCIL

1) You go to meetings and say things like, "The school day should be much SHORTER."

2) You wear a fancy BADGE.

3) You get to stay inside when it's raining.

4) Little kids think you're VERY IMPORTANT.

5) Being a school councillor would really annoy Marcus. (It's worth doing it just for THAT.)

Mr Fullerman explains that part of the lesson today is making a POSTER for YOURSELF, a made-up person OR even a CREATURE. Mark Clump puts up his hand because he doesn't know what Mr Fullerman means...

So he shows us by drawing a POSTER as if he was a GIANT.

VOTE FOR ME - GIANT!
Because I will:
- Scare other GIANTS away.
- Shelter you on school sports days if it rains.
- Eat all the school dinners YOU don't like.

(We all get it now.)

Making our posters for school council elections feels more like an ART class, which I'm very happy about. There's coloured paper, scissors, pens, pencils and all kinds of stuff to use.

129

Me...

Marcus puts up his hand and volunteers to take the register back to the school office, which suits me fine because I get to pick out what paper and pens I want to use.

He's been gone for **AGES** now – not that I mind. It's more peaceful without him around. Marcus has left his LIST about why we should vote for him on his desk. I can't resist quick PEEK while he's NOT here.

Hmmmm ... interesting. There are SO many things I could add – but I don't.

VOTE FOR ME
to be
SCHOOL COUNCILLOR
Marcus Meldrew
(MM for short)
BECAUSE:
I am VERY popular.
I am VERY smart.
I'm good at lots of things.
My unusual hobby
is collecting dinosaurs.
I have nice clear handwriting
(useful).
I would do a GOOD job

I'm going to do a REALLY BIG poster covered with my doodles to make it stand out. I've drawn it in pencil. Now all I need is a black felt-tip to colour it in with. My one has RUN OUT. (I need more pens.) I start using the THIN ➤ black felt-tip, which is the only one I can find.

It's going to take me a LONG time to colour in the WHOLE poster with this thin pen. But it will be WORTH it. When Marcus comes back he's REALLY out of breath.

"You were gone a long time, Marcus," Mr Fullerman says to him.

"Sorry, sir – I had to wait for Mrs Mumble."

Marcus picks out some paper then looks over at my poster and says, "That looks complicated."

"You've been gone a long time," I remind him.

"I got stuck waiting for Mrs Mumble – and **Buster Jones** was in the office too, waiting for Mr Keen."

 "He WAS? Did he say anything to you?"

"Sort of – not much. That's going to take you a long time to colour in," he adds, looking at my poster again.

 "My pen's stopped working. I've only got this thin pen now."

"Here – HAVE THIS **THICK BLACK MARKER PEN.** You can use this."

 "REALLY? Wow, thanks Marcus," I say and I start using it.

It's a really good **MARKER PEN** he's given me.

"This is perfect. It would have taken me **AGES** to finish this off otherwise," I say.

Sometimes Marcus can be the most ANNOYING boy in the **WHOLE** class and then he goes and does something NICE that helps me out. ← Nice

As I'm finishing off colouring in my poster with the good pen, the tannoy system starts to **CRACKLE**.

It's Mr Keen - who sounds a bit STERN.

"OAKFIELD SCHOOL, I AM VERY DISAPPOINTED ONCE AGAIN! MORE GRAFFITI HAS BEEN FOUND. SOMEONE HAS BEEN DEFACING SCHOOL PROPERTY WITH A THICK BLACK MARKER PEN. IF ANYONE KNOWS ANYTHING ABOUT THIS, PLEASE TELL YOUR TEACHER. THANK YOU."

Did Mr Keen just say **THICK BLACK MARKER PEN?**

I think he did.

(133)

"I don't know anything about it," Marcus says but **not** in a very convincing way.

 "Did **YOU** do the graffiti with THIS pen, Marcus?" I ask - because he looks a bit *shifty*.

"No! It wasn't me!"

"Where did you get this pen from, Marcus? I don't want **Mr Keen** thinking **I** drew the graffiti."

Marcus **leans** closer and whispers.
"Shhh - keep your voice down. I'll tell you what happened but you have to keep quiet."

"That depends. Keep going."
So Marcus explains why he gave me the "guilty" pen.

I volunteered to take the register down to the school office. I wanted to be helpful so Mr Fullerman and the class would notice and think I'd be a good school councillor.

 You'll need to do a lot more than THAT.

Very funny... Anyway, Mrs Mumble was BUSY talking on the phone so I had to wait, and GUESS WHO ELSE was waiting to see Mr Keen?

 Who?

Guess...

 Buster Jones.

Correct!

 So what happened next?

Buster told me Mr Keen wanted to talk to him about the graffiti. He said he knew NOTHING about it really LOUDLY, in case Mrs Mumble could hear him.

 Did he?

Then while I was still waiting for **M**rs **M**umble, **Buster** asked if I wanted a PEN. He told me it was a special pen but he didn't need it anymore and I'd be doing him a favour. So I took the pen.

 Didn't you think that was a bit **WEIRD?**

Buster's not easy to say "no" to. Besides, I thought maybe he was being nice to me.

 I thought **YOU** were being NICE as well — not just getting rid of evidence.

OK. I admit it crossed my mind he was giving me the graffiti pen. But you needed a new pen and besides now **M**r **F**ullerman loves your poster.

 How do you know?

He's holding it up.

"Well done, Tom. This is a very good poster. Can everyone see how Tom's used the THICK BLACK MARKER PEN to make his message stand out?"

(They can now.)

I wish Mr Fullerman would stop saying **"THICK BLACK MARKER PEN".** I manage to accidentally on purpose lose it in the class pen box.

Hopefully that pen won't find its way back to me. (No thanks to Marcus.)

My poster does look pretty good, though. Which is something.

PEN BOX

PLAN A B̶ C̶ or is it D?

The NEXT part of my PLAN is to go back to the library (AGAIN) and have a SNEAKY peek in a few more books. My drawing MUST be there ... somewhere. There's no point in taking the **BIG BOOK OF BIRDWATCHING** home now. I take the book and drop it on to my chair, then I *PUSH* the chair under the table to HIDE IT.

No one notices so I head off to the library —*FAST.* Derek's waiting for me at the school gate so I can't be too long.

but when I get there ...

there's A PROBLEM.

COMPUTER CLUB is on and there are LOADS of kids sitting EXACTLY where I want to be.

THEN Ms Lucas spots me and STRAIGHT
AWAY she asks...

- If I'm here for COMPUTER CLUB? (No, miss...)

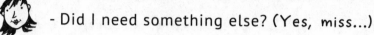   - Did I need something else? (Yes, miss...)

- Do I STILL have the birdwatching book...

(Errr ... NO ... I mean YES.) 😊

I tell Ms Lucas that Derek is keeping it safe for
me while I'm here.

"He's waiting outside. I just need to check out a
few more books." 😊

"I can't let you take another reference book out, Tom,"
she tells me. "You promised me you'd look after the
bird book."

"I REALLY am," I say, nodding.

Ms Lucas might have been a little more convinced...

... if **T**revor Peters hadn't suddenly turned up slightly out of breath and *PUFFING* while **HOLDING THE BOOK!**

"Tom, I've been trying to catch up with you. This book's **HEAVY!**

Mr **F**ullerman said you left it on your chair and you need to bring it HOME with you."

"**D**id I? How did *THAT* happen?"

(Uh-oh.)

Luckily for me **M**s **L**ucas needs to start the COMPUTER CLUB as all the kids are waiting for her. **S**o I PROMISE not to let THIS book out of my SIGHT and manage to convince **M**s **L**ucas that I am a responsible and trustworthy kid who will "look after the birdwatching book and bring it back tomorrow".

"Make sure you do, Tom."

When Derek sees me he says, "You were **AGES**. That book looks **HEAVY**."

"It is, but I have to bring it with me."

As we walk home (slowly in my case)

I start to tell Derek how Marcus

gave me the pen **Buster** had used to do the GRAFFITI.

No way! Derek says.

"THEN I drew my **WHOLE** ENTIRE school council VOTE FOR ME poster with it."

Did you hear Mr Keen's announcement?

"Did I!"

Then Derek starts doing a **WEIRD** face as I tell him, "Having **Buster's** PEN and listening to Mr Keen talking about GRAFFITI was REALLY AWKWARD."

"No. This is going to be awkward," Derek says.

"Hey, GATESY! Marcus Meldrew said he
gave you my pen and I need it back."
Buster Jones has caught up with me and Derek and
it's TOO LATE TO HIDE! I **PANIC** and tell him

the truth.

"I DID have it, but it's in the class pen
box now. Sorry, Buster."

"Tom didn't know it was your pen,"
Derek adds.

(Good point. Thanks, Derek.)

Buster SCOWLS, then says, "That's OK – I have
other pens. Just as long as you haven't
said anything about YOU KNOW WHAT."

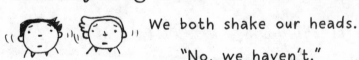 We both shake our heads.

"No, we haven't."

"Good. I'll see you around, Gatesy
and Pingle."

Then just when we think he's about to go,
Buster adds,

"what's with the **BIG BOOK OF BIRDWATCHING,**

Gatesy?"

I'm <u>not</u> going to tell him about my missing drawing

so I just say,

"Well — I thought I'd left something inside,

but it wasn't there and now I have to

take the book home with me."

"Annoying. Oh well."

We watch **Buster** walk off down the road.

"Do you think he's going to call me Pingle all

the time now?"

"Yep — I do."

Back at home I'm about to ⟳DUMp my bag and book, when I hear VOICES.

Dad's in the kitchen having a cup of tea with Uncle Kevin, which is GOOD NEWS because

TEA = BISCUITS. So I go and join them.

"I thought I'd check their house was OK while they're away," Uncle Kevin is saying.

"It looks like they're enjoying themselves," Dad says while reading a NEW postcard from THE FOSSILS.

"I could do with a holiday," Dad adds.

"Me too," I agree as I put down my BIG book and bag.

"We always PLAN our holidays WAY in advance. We're very organized like that," Uncle Kevin tells Dad, who doesn't answer him.

"Help yourself to a biscuit, Tom. Good day at school?"

Before I can answer, Uncle Kevin notices the book.

"Look at that! Do you like birdwatching, Tom?" Uncle Kevin asks.

I am **about** to say, "Not really," when Uncle Kevin starts looking through the book and telling me ALL kinds of things about birds.

"Do you know what you're called if you go birdwatching?"

(Dad is rolling his eyes.)

Here we go.

"YES – you're a TWIT... I mean, you're a TWITCHER," I say, which makes Dad LAUGH.

Ha! Ha! Ha!

"We used to get taken birdwatching by our dad, didn't we, Frank?"

"Yes, we did. You always had the proper clothes AND I seem to remember you TOOK my best binoculars."

"I don't think so.

I would have had my OWN pair."

145

Before Uncle Kevin goes home he says,
"Hey, Tom, I could take you
birdwatching when you come over at the
weekend if you like?"

I try to say, "Oh ... I'm not sure..."

But Uncle Kevin doesn't really listen.
"It will be *FUN*! I can show you all
kinds of interesting things."

"HA! That'll be a first then," Dad laughs.

Very funny, Frank.

Once Uncle Kevin has left, Dad starts
telling me HIS side of the birdwatching story.
"Just for the record, he DID pinch my
binoculars. I remember that very well."

"If you say so, Dad," I say between mouthfuls.

Since I've LUGGED this BIRDWATCHING book home
with me, I might as well have another look at it.
I carry it up to my room and
go through EVERY page
(just in case).
The **BAD NEWS** IS: 🙁
My drawing definitely isn't there
(but I knew that already).

THE GOOD NEWS is I know a lot more
about birdwatching (which isn't <u>REALLY</u> good
news, but it will have to do for now as I still
have to work on PLAN E for school tomorrow).
In my HEAD, EVERYTHING goes smoothly:

1. Avoid **Bully Buster.** (I try to do that anyway.)
2. Take the BIRD book back to library.
3. FIND the RIGHT book (the one WITH my drawing).
4. Keep hold of the drawing. (For ever.)
5. CHEER and high five. (A lot!)

PLAN E

My plan doesn't EXACTLY start off like it's supposed to...

1. I WAKE UP LATE. —YAWN   Mum and Dad shout at me to "Hurry up! Get going."

2. I miss Derek, who's already left for school.

3. I have to walk on my own AND carry the **HEAVY** birdwatching book the whole way, which slows me down even more. (I'm late for school.)

4. The FIRST person I see at school is Buster Jones. (I hide behind the book.) THE BIG BOOK OF

5. I have to apologize to Mr Fullerman for me being late. (Still holding the book.) Sorry, sir. THE BIG BOOK OF BIRDWATCHING

Then Mr Fullerman actually SUGGESTS that I

should take the book straight down to the library,

which is BRILLIANT because that means I

can get my drawing

RIGHT NOW.

(I'm back on track with my plan.)

Norman waves at me but I can't wave back as the

book is so **HEAVY.**

Ms Lucas is VERY pleased to see me and to

get the book back in one piece.

"Well done, Tom. I hope it was useful for you. You've been

here a lot recently, haven't you?"

(She doesn't mention the drawing – so that's good.)

"I need another book, Ms Lucas," I explain.

Ms Lucas seems a bit surprised.

"Another BIRD BOOK? Is there a school project

on birdwatching at the moment?"

 "Not that I know of."

"I just wondered because Buster Jones was here this

morning and he did exactly the same thing as you. He

was looking through the other copy of the birdwatching

book."

 Did Ms Lucas just say ...

"The OTHER COPY OF THE

BIRDWATCHING BOOK?"

"Yes, Tom, we have two copies of that book in the library

– that's why I let you take this one out."

"AND **BUSTER** WAS READING IT?"

I ask, because THAT seems a bit ODD.

"I was as surprised as you!"

Then Ms Lucas tells me that he seemed to be

really enjoying it.

"He was LAUGHING a LOT. I had to

ask him to keep it down. I thought it was

a bit strange because I've read that book and

it's NOT funny at all."

"Is the book still here?" I ask her.

"Yes – over there." Ms Lucas points it out. I RUSH

over to take a look myself. It's exactly the SAME

book as the one I've just taken back. I go through

it PAGE by PAGE.

"No ... no ... not there ...

no ... no ... no ... no ... no..."

I keep going.

151

But then I come across a bit of paper STUCK in the middle of the book. It LOOKS like it's been *RIPPED* out in a hurry. I recognize the handwriting because it's <u>MY</u> handwriting! I think **Buster Jones** has FOUND my drawing.

(Evidence)

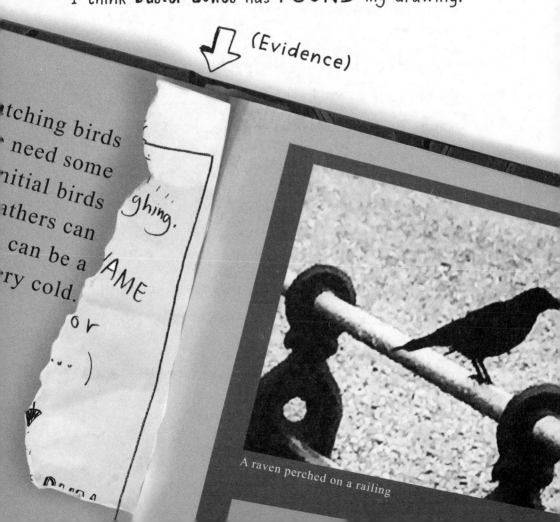

tching birds
need some
nitial birds
athers can
can be a
ry cold.

ghing.

AME

o r

...)

A raven perched on a railing

(NONE of that was in my PLAN at all. No
wonder **Buster** was laughing at the book.)

"Did you find what you were looking for, Tom?"
Ms Lucas asks.

I take out the scrap of paper.

"Or can I find you another book on birds?" she adds.

"No ... what I want isn't here at all NOW."

I tell her.

 - for failure.

That's what this is.)

I walk back to class and

decide to put PLAN G

into action.

PLAN ...
GET MY
DRAWING
BACK!

→

TOP FIVE things that are NOT EASY for me to do right now:

1. Get my drawing BACK from **Buster**.

2. Not **PANIC** THAT **Buster** HAS MY DRAWING.

3. **FIND** **Buster** AND TAKE BACK MY DRAWING.

4. Listen to Marcus (chat.) (AT ALL.)

5. Be enthusiastic about going to see the cousins at the weekend.

I tell Derek at lunch break that I think **Buster** has my drawing and show him the SCRAP of paper. "If he has your drawing, he's not going to just HAND it back to you, is he?" (It's a good point.)

"Maybe we could sneak it back from him when he's NOT looking."

"HOW?"  I ask, because I have no idea at all.

"Follow me."

We go and find **Buster Jones**, who's standing around the school grounds. When I say "FIND", I mean we can see him from a safe distance (behind a wall).

Buster has his bag with him, and as we watch, he takes out WHAT LOOKS like a piece of paper.

"What's THAT?" **D**erek says to me.

"It could be my drawing," I say.

We try and get closer to have a proper look.

Closer ...

and closer. The trouble is ...

Caretaker Stan is keeping an EYE on us.

He's wondering what we're up to, I can tell.

So we make our way back to where we came from and leave **Buster** with my drawing.

"It's like we're in a BIG COMPUTER game, isn't it?" Derek says.

I know EXACTLY what he means.

Bully Buster is the Graffiti Kid who's stolen <u>MY</u> drawing. I have to get it back when he's not looking.

Caretaker STAN is on the lookout. <u>He</u>'s trying to CATCH the Graffiti Kid RED-HANDED. But what if he thinks it's  who did the graffiti? And if he catches me before I find my drawing and the BELL goes IT'S...

GAME OVER.

Caretaker Stan has been making a SPECIAL effort to look out for ANYONE who is behaving SUSPICIOUSLY around school. I saw him looking VERY closely at the PEN marks on my school councillor poster as if he was trying to remember WHERE he'd seen <u>THAT</u> PEN before.

mmmmm.

I haven't done ANYTHING wrong but every time I SEE Caretaker Stan it feels like I've got an [arrow > over my head that says:

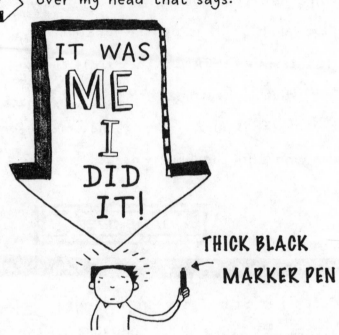

IT WAS
ME
I
DID
IT!

THICK BLACK
MARKER PEN

It probably hasn't helped that I've been holding a pen or doing some drawing the last few times he's SPOTTED me.

Pens

I love doodling and drawing!

Caretaker Stan

Chalk

Tom

But HEY! Thanks to Buster's pen at least my school council election poster looks pretty good. There's only a few days to go before the VOTE and all the posters are up around the school. (Some are more convincing than others...)

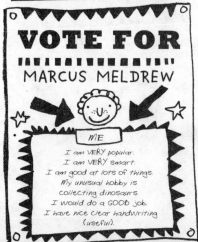

COUNTDOWN to school election

We get to choose THREE kids to go through to the FINAL from our class. Then the whole school votes for who the school councillors will be.

(Who knows?)

I'm still wondering if **Buster** really took my drawing when, at break time, Derek comes _running_ over to find me. He's shouting,

Thinking →

"*Tom! Tom! Tom!* I've seen the drawing of YOU KNOW WHO. He's got it! **Buster** has your drawing!"

"Really – are you SURE?" I say.

Derek says it's DEFINITELY my drawing.

"While **Buster** was playing football I took a PEEK in his bag and your drawing was THERE - I SAW it!"

"Why didn't you TAKE it?" I ask. "I didn't think of THAT."

Derek and I decide to go BACK and grab the drawing while **Buster** is still BUSY. THIS could be it - FINALLY! Norman wants to come too. He says he can JUMP around or just stand in everyone's way if we need him to.

(THAT'S PLAN G)

We creep towards **Buster's** bag while he is playing football.

Buster

Drawing

There are a few kids standing around, and every time someone looks up we F R E E Z E.

Standing around the bag trying not to look like we're up to anything dodgy isn't easy. Norman starts waving his arms around while I *LEAN* down towards it.

"I can see it!" I tell Derek who's keeping a LOOKOUT.

I'm about to TAKE my drawing when the football comes FLYING through the air RIGHT towards us.

Norman LEAPS up and shouts,

SAVE!

Now EVERYONE, including Buster, is looking over at us.

"Gatesy! Gatesy! I want to TALK to you."

(So much for Norman distracting attention AWAY from us.)

I FREEZE until I realize that **Buster** is now *RUNNING* towards me.

"Quick, let's go!" **D**erek says.

Norman throws back the football and we all leg it as fast as we can.

Mr **S**procket is standing by the school door ready to blow the whistle for end of break.

So we all run straight into school to get away from **Buster**. I'm out of breath and PUFFING.

"That was close!" I say to **D**erek before he goes to his lesson.

"At least you got your drawing BACK."

"That was FUN!" **N**orman adds.

"There's only one problem..." I tell them.

163

"I didn't get my drawing."

(PLAN H it is then.)

PLAN H

(Doesn't work.)

OI!

← DISGUISE

PLAN I

(Isn't a great success either.)

Over the next two days I really TRY to get my drawing back. But NOTHING WORKS and Buster STILL has it in his bag. Which is not ideal. I'm not very happy about this ... at all. 🙁

There is ONE bit of good news though. The first round of voting for the school councillors has taken place and me, Norman and Julia Morton have made it through to the final. YES!

"Well done to everyone who took part. You three now need to write a speech for when the whole school gets to vote. Are you UP FOR THAT?"

(I forgot about that bit.)

Marcus didn't get through - you can tell just by looking at him. He perks up a lot when Mr Fullerman mentions ECO COUNCILLORS.

"If anyone wants to put their names forward to be an ECO COUNCILLOR, let me know. It's a very important part of school life."

(There's one person who does for sure.)

THE WEEKEND VISIT TO THE COUSINS'

We've had MORE postcards from **THE FOSSILS**
and they've sent some photos too.
They look like they're having a lot of fun.

There are LOUD noises coming from downstairs
that WAKE me up really early in the morning. I feel
a bit **GRUMPY** about this ... until I smell
something that's a bit like pancakes.

I get dressed and go downstairs as FAST as I can and discover that it IS **PANCAKES!** Which cheers me up and is an excellent start to the day after all. Delia must have smelt them cooking because she's up earlier than usual as well.

Mum and Dad are very busy this morning. "Isn't this **NICE?** A lovely family breakfast together," Mum says, just before she **burns** one of the pancakes and sets the FIRE ALARM OFF.

Dad has to stand on a chair to push the **STOP** button. He puts his hand on the ceiling to STEADY himself and manages to knock over a CUP of coffee with his FOOT. It spills all over the table and on some of the pancakes too. I SAVE my pancake but the others are a bit soggy. Dad looks for the paper towels to clean up the mess with.

BEEP!
BEEP!
BEEP!

SAVE!

"We've run out of paper towels. And loads of other things too. I'll have toast instead," Mum says before she realizes there isn't any of that either.

"There's not much milk if you want cereal," Dad adds helpfully just as Delia takes the LAST bit of chocolate spread to put on HER pancake. So I call her a SNAKE! for not leaving me any for MY pancake. Mum tells me off and says, "That's enough, you two! We'll do some shopping at some point. I don't know when."

Then while Dad wipes up the coffee with a tea towel, I notice something on the ceiling that looks like a SPIDER.

So I say SPIDER!

Delia JUMPS (and I LAUGH).

Mum says, "Where?"

"Up there." ⬆ I point.

"That's not a **SPIDER** – that's my handprint from when I turned off the alarm. Sorry," Dad says.

"Oh well, that's OK then. A grubby handprint on the ceiling!" Mum doesn't sound very happy at all.

"I'll clean it off when I have time," Dad tells her.

"That will never happen then. So much for a nice family breakfast," Mum sighs.

"Shouldn't you all be at Uncle Kevin's house by now?" Delia reminds everyone.

I'd forgotten about THAT. Mum rushes off to get ready and Dad tells me they'll drop me off FIRST.

"Have a nice time – I know you will," Delia says as we leave the house.

In the car Mum and Dad are worried that Delia might be planning to have LOADS of her friends over while they're out.

"It's happened before," Mum says as she puts on her make-up.

And Delia's a SNAKE, I say from the back seat (because she took the last bit of chocolate spread).

Mum gives me a LOOK. "ENOUGH of the 'snake', please," Mum sighs. Then she tells Dad to go the QUICK way.

"I'm TRYING," he says while STOPPING and STARTING all the time.
It makes reading my comic tricky as well.

"For GOODNESS' sake!" Mum keeps muttering.
When we finally get to
Uncle Kevin's, Mum jumps out of the car and takes me to the house.

I'm **TRYING** to tell her she has SMUDGED her make-up when Uncle Kevin opens the door and does it for me.

"Hello ... whoa, what's with the WILD make-up, Rita? In a hurry, were you?"

Mum wipes her eyes, which makes it worse. She tells "It's Frank's driving. The traffic was awful," she explains. "Thanks so much for having Tom. We'll see you later. Now be good."

"I will!" Uncle Kevin jokes.
Mum runs back to the car and tries to fix her make-up as Dad drives off.

"Right, I've got a SURPRISE for you, Tom."
Which is a good start. Today's going to be OK after all. I like surprises ...

(most of them.)

The cousins
BOO

We go into the house and everyone seems pleased to see me, which is nice. Aunty Alice asks,

"How's that lovely sister of yours?"

It takes me a few seconds to work out who she's talking about.

"Do you mean Delia?"

She does.

"Grumpy as always."

Then Uncle Kevin says in a really LOUD, excited VOICE, "It's GREAT you're here, Tom, because now I can say ...

HANDS UP if you want to come on a VERY SPECIAL ADVENTURE!"

I put my hand UP because I like the sound of an ☆ADVENTURE☆.

Then I notice the cousins' hands haven't moved at all.

Confused

 So I put mine down. Uncle Kevin says, "That's sorted then. You're all coming."

"Apart from me," Aunty Alice points out.

 "And us," the cousins add.

"You're both going," Aunty Alice tells them.

"Don't you want to come?" I ask the cousins while Uncle Kevin goes off to get something.

"Trust us, Tom, birdwatching isn't much of an adventure."

"BIRDWATCHING?" I'm wondering if it's too late to change my mind when Uncle Kevin comes back and gives me a PRESENT.

"Here you go, Tom. Something for the special adventure."

"Thanks, Uncle Kevin!" I say as I open the box.

"Binoculars!"

"They used to be mine, but I thought you might like them. We can use them on our trip. The boys have their own already, don't you?"

"We do," they sigh.

"They're brilliant, Uncle Kevin," I say, because I really do like them!

Uncle Kevin tells us, "I'll be back in FIVE; just got to get a few things together." While he's gone the cousins tell me "We have a SURPRISE for you too, Tom.

"Stay here – we'll call you."

I fall for it
EVERY TIME.
(You'd think I'd remember.)

After playing their TRICK (again) the
cousins tell me they have a few things to bring
birdwatching as well.

"We have to hide them from Dad,
though." They're waving around a couple of bird
pictures cut out and stuck on card like puppets. I'm
confused.

"What are they for?"

"It's our emergency jay-bird sighting," they explain.
"Dad won't go home until we've SEEN some kind of
bird. SO that's when we bring out one of THESE –
see, like this." They demonstrate by shaking them
around and making TWEETING noises.

"That actually works?" I wonder, because
                    it's NOT that convincing.

"Trust us, it works," they say, hiding the birds as
Uncle Kevin comes back...

He's wearing a very odd jacket.
"This one's yours, Tom. It'll help you
blend in with the foliage so you don't
stand out so much."

(You can say that again.)
"We'll head to the wood near that small river.
There's plenty of wildlife to look at there."

Aunty Alice suggests we have LUNCH before
we go, which sounds like a good idea to ME.
But then she adds, "It's TUNA casserole, is that OK
for you Tom?"

"Ummmmm..."

(My face gives away how I'm feeling.)

Luckily Uncle Kevin wants to save time so we
bring sandwiches with us, which I am VERY
HAPPY about.

YES!

THE SPECIAL ADVENTURE BIRDWATCHING

(Sort of)

When Dad's not around, Uncle Kevin likes to tell me stories about when they were both kids.

"He's ALWAYS been clumsy."

"He USED to have hair!"

Today he's telling me the binoculars story.

Dad's told me this story before so I say,

"Dad he put BOOT POLISH on the eyepieces to stop you from pinching them."

"I just borrowed them,"

Uncle Kevin explains.

"Dad said the marks round your eyes lasted a month. He laughed a LOT when he told me THAT."

The cousins are LAUGHING now too.

"They lasted a week. Typical of your dad to EXAGGERATE."

"Dad said you looked like a panda."

(I'm laughing now too.)

"Shhhh, you lot – you'll scare the birds away."

I get the feeling that Uncle Kevin doesn't want to talk about the binoculars any more.

We start doing a bit of birdwatching and my new binoculars are brilliant.

← Close-up of sparrow

Uncle Kevin tells us a few interesting* birdwatching facts as we walk. (Some ARE more interesting than others.) Thanks to the **BIG BOOK OF BIRDWATCHING**, I know quite a lot about birds already.

* See page 225 for some (sort of) interesting birdwatching facts.

We're still walking when Uncle Kevin says
"Shhhhh ... LOOK OVER THERE!"

We pick up our binoculars and I can see ...

NOTHING.

NOTHING at all.

So we wait.

Then we wait a bit more.

And a bit more on top of that.

"Birdwatching is all about being patient,"
Uncle Kevin is telling us.

"... and being really bored," the cousins
whisper to me.

"Keep nice and still – I think there's a JAY over
there," Uncle Kevin tells us.

But ALL I can hear now is our stomachs rumbling.

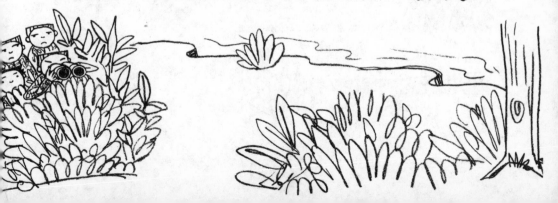

The rumbling gets so loud, Uncle Kevin says we should eat lunch now. Which is a great idea – until I see what it is.

"Tuna sandwich, Tom?" he says. The cousins are happy to eat mine while I eat everything else on offer.

"The GREAT thing about birdwatching is that some days you might not see a lot of birds, but it's the EXCITEMENT of what's out there. So let's keep looking." Uncle Kevin keeps a birdwatching notebook so he can write down what he sees.

"How long do we have to stay here for?" the cousins ask.

"As long as it takes," Uncle Kevin tells us. The cousins give me a LOOK.

Operation FAKE BIRD goes into action.
I keep Uncle Kevin chatting while they disappear
and place the birds just far enough away that
they look real.

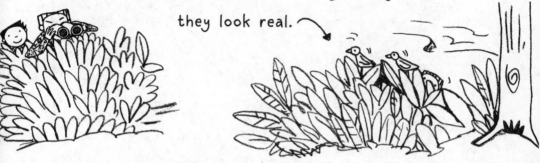

"L⊙⊙k, Uncle Kevin, over there!" I tell him.
He's SO happy we've finally got to see such
"Beautiful birds! Wasn't that fascinating?"

"It was," I say as the cousins sneak back   "Amazing"
and agree with EVERYTHING he says.

We stay for a while longer and
                Uncle Kevin keeps looking...

"Next time we come birdwatching we should get
up REALLY early to catch the best birds."
(I'm thinking, *Next time?*)

Eventually Uncle Kevin says we can go home. "What a shame we didn't see more birds – but there's just not that many around today," he adds.

Mum and Dad are LATE picking me up from
the cousins, so I have to stay for dinner too.
The TUNA casserole is finished

(which is a RELIEF),

so we have noodles and listen to Uncle Kevin
talking about the "jay bird" sighting and how
"amazing" they were.
Aunty Alice wonders why me and the
cousins are all laughing.

"No reason," we all say.
When Mum and Dad arrive Uncle Kevin tells
them about the "jay bird" sighting too.
It's hard to keep a straight face.

I say, "Thank you for having me," instead,
which helps.
In the car driving home Mum asks me if I had a
good time.
"It was a lot more FUN than I
thought it was going to be." (Which is true.)

When we get back home something

UNBELIEVABLE

has happened. Something that's NEVER happened

before. Mum and Dad are STUNNED.

(I'm surprised too.)

DELIA has only gone and ... MADE DINNER.

(It's just pizza - but she's never done it before.)

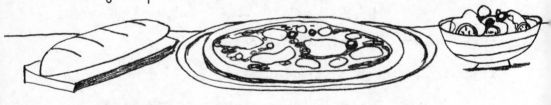

She's even laid the table and made SALAD too.

SURPRISE!
I know you've
been busy parents,
so I thought you'd
like some food.
(No slugs or crunchy
frog, Tom!)
                    Delia X

Mum and Dad won't STOP going

on about Delia making them

dinner. I've eaten already so

it's a good time to go to bed.

COUNTDOWN to election week

THIS WEEK

It's ALL happening this week at school. :(

The TEST.

The school council election.

AND PARENTS' EVENING

(something I'd forgotten about)

THE FOSSILS are coming home as well. They sent us
ANOTHER postcard that has made us all think that
Granny Mavis might be keen to try out a few new
dishes on us at some point.

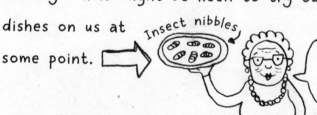

Insect nibbles

Special insects rolled in seeds and deep fried. Yum!

---

* One hand up means I've heard that story before.
Two hands up means I've heard that story before
AND I <u>don't</u> want to hear it again.

I've managed **NOT** to think about how **Buster** still has my drawing. I just hope he doesn't leave it somewhere or do anything silly with it!

← School notice board

When I go into class it's all a bit more RELAXED for the TEST this time.

Mr Fullerman is even playing music as we come into class - which is quite nice.

We sit down and are ready to...

TURN OVER THE PAPER AND START YOUR TEST."

So that's what I do.

The **WHOLE** TEST goes surprisingly well (no itchy foot this time).

CALM

When it's over, Mr Fullerman tells us we'll find out how we did at...

PARENTS' EVENING

(Like that's something to look forward to.)

"Nothing to worry about at all," he adds.

PLAN A b c d e F G h I j K L
M n O P Q r s t U V W x Y
(I've lost track.)

Z

Me, Derek, Norman, Solid and Brad are all hanging out together in the school grounds after the TEST.

"I'm glad THAT'S over," Norman says.

"Me too," I agree. Then Derek asks me if I've worked out my SPEECH for the **school council election...**

"SPEECH - WHAT SPEECH?"

(Something else I'd forgotten about.)

"I've done MINE," Norman says. Then he stands on bench and gives us a demonstration of his carefully thought-out speech...

"WHAT do we WANT?

Then here's where YOU have to shout back at me ... CHIPS!"

So we all shout out, "CHIPS!"

"When do we want them?" "NOW!"

"That's my speech really. I read out a list and do lots of jumping and shouting."

(It's still better than my speech, that's for sure.)

I stand on the bench and have a think about WHAT to say. Up here I can see right over to the other side of the school grounds to where kids are playing football and that's when I SPOT Buster JONES.

WHO SUDDENLY LOOKS

RIGHT BACK AT ME!

(Or do<u>es</u> he?) I'm quite far away so I stay still and keep looking at him to see what he's going to do. Go back to playing football? Turn around?

Or START running

TOWARDS ME! Uh-oh!

I shout, "Quick, I have to HIDE. Buster's coming over. Tell him I've GONE somewhere else. Don't mention my drawing!" I look round and there's just enough time to hide behind a plant pot.

Buster comes over and asks everyone,

"Where's GATESY?"

"Never heard of him," Norman says, which is a silly thing to say because of course he knows who I am!

"Oh, Tom's gone back to class. He was in a hurry." Derek says.

"Well tell him I REALLY need to see him. It's important, OK, Pingle?"

Derek nods as Buster starts to walk away. (Phew, that was close. It's NEVER a good thing if Buster wants to "TALK" to you.)

I'm waiting for the coast to be clear when Marcus Meldrew taps me on the shoulder.

"What are you doing hiding there? TOM...? TOM...?"

"Go away, Marcus – please."

"Why are you hiding, Tom?"

He won't go. So I decide to make a RUN for it just as Buster hears my NAME.

"I'm OFF!"

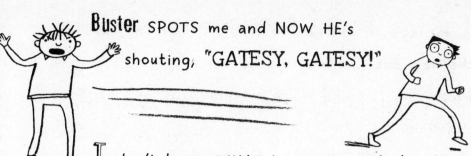

Buster SPOTS me and NOW HE's shouting, "GATESY, GATESY!"

I don't know WHAT he wants and I'm not going to hang around to find out. I manage to run back to my class just as the bell goes. I'm OUT of BREATH but at least **Buster** can't bother me here.

AMY PORTER sits down and says, "You look RED and a bit puffed out, Tom."

"Yup," I say, because I can't talk properly yet. I get the feeling **Buster** is going to keep looking for me. I might have to do a lot more hiding and running (or both) to keep out of his way.

I manage to AVOID **Buster Jones** for the rest of the day. But it's the rest of the week that gets a bit tricky. It's like we're playing HIDE and SEEK all the time.

Me hiding in the trees

Cloakroom

Under a table   Phew

I'm starting to get a bit FED UP trying to AVOID **Buster.**

Derek tells me I should find out what he wants.

"You can't KEEP running off and hiding, Tom. It's CRAZY!"

Derek's RIGHT.

I'VE HAD ENOUGH.

I decide I'm going to go up to

Buster ONCE AND FOR ALL

and ask for MY drawing BACK.

THEN I'LL FIND OUT what he

wants. NO more hiding

for me! I'm going to find

him ... RIGHT ...

... after the school

election speeches.

I'll do it then.

School council
speeches

After I saw Norman's CHIP speech, I thought I should PRACTISE what I'm going to say. I did it at home, which was FINE until Delia heard me and started putting me off.

Ha! Ha! Ha! Ha!

What are you doing?

Derek came round and he told me I was doing fine, so I IGNORED Delia.

Right now I'm trying to ignore Marcus Meldrew, who wants to know if I'm nervous about making a speech in front of the

WHOLE ENTIRE SCHOOL.

"I wasn't until you reminded me, Marcus," I say.

We all go into the hall - and YES the WHOLE school is there. Mr Keen gives us another TALK about (DEFACING school property.) He says there's been no more graffiti and he HOPES it's going to stay that way. Caretaker Stan is nodding his head. I make sure I don't look at him for too long.

THE FIRST SPEECHES START.

The idea of a much shorter school day gets a BIG CHEER for the first speaker. Next Julia Morton tells everyone they should vote for her because she is:

* VERY organized. ———> (True.)

* Can TALK to teachers. ——> (True.)

* Kids like her. ————7 (True.)

* She'll bring in ... CAKE FRIDAY! (Wow!)

(She gets my vote and a BIG round of applause.)

There are a few more kids from different classes that make speeches before Norman does a great job with his CHIP speech.

Now it's MY turn. I've got a copy of my poster to READ from.

"Hello, everyone. I'd like to be YOUR school councillor for LOTS of reasons. For a START, Monday will no longer be the day that everyone dreads. Monday will be..."

I'm about to say ☆FUN☆ DAY when I SPOT Buster Jones looking STRAIGHT at me. He's saying, "I HAVE YOUR DRAWING."

I stop talking ... and start saying, "Errrrr, I'm going to make, errrrrrr... Sorry, where was I?"

I manage to finish my speech. But Buster really put me off. It wasn't great.

THIS IS GETTING STUPID.

When I get back to class, Marcus says, "What happened to you?" and I say, "Nothing - I just have to go and sort something out."

And that's what I do.

At lunchtime.

Derek comes with me because he wants me to sort this out too. "You'll be fine, Tom - I'm here."

I can see **Buster** chatting to some kids. I walk over (GULP) and say, "**Buster Jones...**"

Before I can change my mind he turns round.

"GATESY! I've been looking for YOU."

"Me too." ←— My voice goes all small.

"Did you leave a drawing inside a book?"

 "Yes."

Then **Buster** says...

HUH? I wasn't expecting **Buster** to say THAT. Derek's SHOCKED too.

 "I saw you hide something in that BIRDWATCHING BOOK in the library. I guessed you were looking for it, so I wanted to help you get it back. You don't want to end up in trouble like me! And thanks for not saying anything about <u>my</u> little drawing."

Then **Buster** hands me back my drawing. "Hang on — one more look," he says and starts laughing again. Derek gets to see it too.

"It was worth the wait!" He laughs too. We still can't believe **Buster** was actually NICE

and helpful!

(Who knew?)

PARENTS' EVENING

Groan

TOP FIVE REASONS PARENTS' EVENING CAN BE TRICKY

1. Parents' dodgy outfits.

2. Teachers talking about me.

3. Parents talking about me.

4. Teachers telling parents things you don't want them to know.

5. Parents telling teachers things you don't want them to know.

Lose the hat, Dad.

He gets distracted...

He gets distracted... A LOT.

He didn't do all his homework.

Tom said he had NO homework.

I have to ask Dad to lose the sunglasses before we go into PARENTS' EVENING. (Mum agrees with me.)

Ridiculous!

OK OK

Mr Fullerman smiles and greets us saying,

"Lovely to see you both – and you, Tom." (I'm not sure that's really true.)

They have a general chat about me while I keep quiet. But THEN my school planner gets a mention.

Uh-oh.

"I'm guessing you didn't write these comments about Tom, Mr and Mrs Gates?"

Interesting

(I've been rumbled.)

Whoops!

The next thing that comes up is my school TEST result.

"Remarkable IMPROVEMENT, Tom! Well done. Almost 100% better than before."

"It was all down to NOT having an ITCHY foot, sir," I say, which makes everyone look confused.

"And the extra study I did," I add.

(205)

PARENTS' EVENING goes OK.

Hero

"Well done, Tom." Mum and Dad are very pleased with me – despite my "extra" school planner comments. "I only wrote them because you were **SO** busy. I thought I was helping," I tell Mum and Dad, (Which is sort of true.)

We're walking out of school past the glass cabinet with all the teachers' photos in. Buster's handiwork has all gone now – or that's what I thought. Mum says, "Gosh, since when has **Mr Keen** had a moustache like that?"

Uh-oh ... Buster's been at it again!

(Mrs Nap doesn't look too good either.)

SLEEPOVER and BAND PRACTICE at DEREK'S HOUSE - AT LAST!

Yeah!

HERE ARE MY TOP FIVE REASONS TO HAVE A SLEEPOVER

1. **E**xcellent snacks.
    Mum added this

2. **C**hance to write brilliant **NEW SONGS**.

3. **H**aving a really good **LAUGH** with my friends.
    Ha! Ha! Ha! Ha!

4. **D**elia is out of my way.

5. **S**taying AWAKE really **LATE**.
    Not Sleepy

We've been waiting **AGES** for this sleepover. Derek has everything planned out, and we're doing BAND PRACTICE first. We all have ideas for new songs that we talk about <u>first</u> (in-between snacks).

"Writing songs isn't easy, is it?" Derek says. "We could do another cover song if we can think of a good one."

Norman jumps up and says, "Hey – I almost forgot! I brought my new instrument and I WROTE a new song to play you. Do you want to hear it?"

"Of course we do! Why didn't you tell us earlier?" I say.

Norman goes downstairs to get the new instrument. Derek and I wonder what it is.

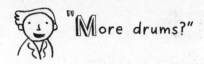 "More drums?"

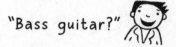 "Bass guitar?"

 "UKULELE!"

"OK!"

 "GREAT!" Norman tells us, "My song's a bit like my school council election speech."

(Which sounds interesting.)

He's about to start playing it for us when IN COMES DEREK'S DAD, Mr Fingle. "HI, BOYS! I have some VERY exciting NEWS. Can you guess what it is?"

"Is it about an OLD BAND by any chance, Dad?" Derek asks him.

"How did you guess? It's VERY exciting!"

 Derek sighs. "What is it then?"

"Our next-door neighbour – who is in **Plastic Cup** – told me they are

REUNITING!
ISN'T THAT AMAZING!"

"Not really." Derek isn't impressed.
"Dad, we're in the middle of a band practice!"

"Norman's written a NEW song. He's going to play it for us now," I tell him.

"Well done, Norman! Mind if I stay and listen?"

"Just don't say anything ... will you?"

"I'm ready when you are!" Norman tells us as he gets ready to play.
"It's called ... 'THE SCHOOL DINNER BLUES',
and it goes like this..."

(Good title!)

THE SCHOOL DINNER
BLUES

YUCK!

When the bell goes for lunch
I'm just hoping and yearning
For something that's tasty
And not stomach churning

YUCK!

It's not much to ask
All I want on a plate
Is food that I LOVE
Not food that I HATE

YEAH!

I've got the school dinner blues
And it's making me sad
All the meals I wish
That I'd never had

Close my eyes and imagine

While licking my lips

That today is the day

They'll be serving up

CHIPS!

CHIPS!

CHIPS!

Vegetarian treat

Chips are the one thing I'm happy to eat

Chips are my favourite, if not EVERYDAY

A portion of chips

Makes a bad day OK

The cooks in the kitchen
Specialize in a dish
Made from leftover scraps
Of the ugliest fish

There's Vera who serves
With a smile and a whistle
As she spoons out the mince
Which is mostly just gristle

Slop...

Do you want mashed potato?
Have one scoop or two
It's the colour of stone
And the texture of glue

(Chorus...)

CLUNK

$\mathbb{I}$t's such a good song ...

... We can't stop singing it.

Chips! ♫ Chips! Chips!

School Councillors AND

Eco Councillors

The school councillors are already getting to work on some changes in school. There will be a **non-uniform day** next term, which should be fun (maybe).

And there's a competition to design a school mascot, because Oakfield School doesn't have one. All the eco councillors have been chosen as well, and Marcus has been picked. He won't stop going on about it now, showing me his badge all the time.

"Do you like my badge, Tom? I'm an eco councillor, you know."

"I know, Marcus. What do you do?"

"Eco councillors SAVE THE PLANET, he tells me, which is a good thing to do...

Here's Marcus at breaktime, saving the planet one crisp packet at a time.

(I'm not sure being an "ECO councillor" is exactly what Marcus thought it was going to be...) He's doing a good job though!

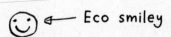 ← Eco smiley

Tom Gates' Glossary

(Which means explanations for stuff
that might sound a bit ODD.)

A4 paper — It's a paper size
(BIGGER than letter size 8½ x 11).

= trash cans.

BINS   BIN

Biscuits = cookies.

Yum!

Caramel wafers: 'Excellent' biscuits (cookies)
covered in
chocolate with layers of
caramel and wafer inside.

WAFERS

Chips are French fries.

Crisps: Chips

Crisps

DAFT = crazy

Dodgy = something that's a bit ODD or wrong.
Maybe slightly peculiar or not quite right. For
instance: That apple looks a bit Dodgy.
That monster looks
a bit dodgy. ←(worm)

Football is another word for soccer.

 Leg it = run away

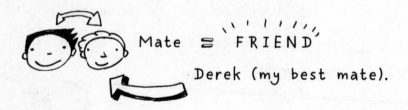 Mate = FRIEND
Derek (my best mate).

MERITS are special POINTS or STARS
awarded by your teacher for excellent
work.

Birdwatching Facts

(Sort of interesting)

How many birds can you see?

(Answer on page 230.)

What's the fastest-moving bird?

Peregrine Falcon diving at 200mph (320 km/h).

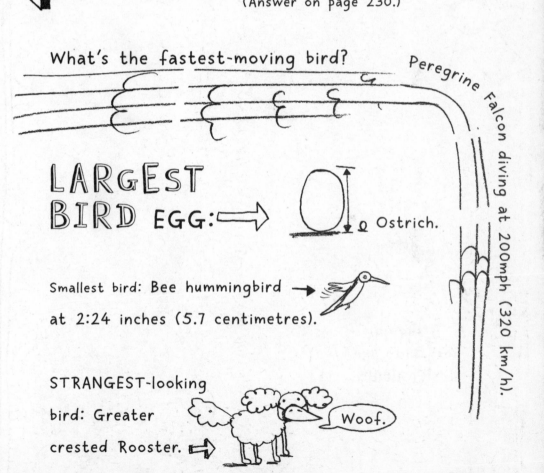

LARGEST BIRD EGG: ➡ 𝜚 Ostrich.

Smallest bird: Bee hummingbird ➡

at 2:24 inches (5.7 centimetres).

STRANGEST-looking bird: Greater crested Rooster. ➡

Woof.

If I'd known how to make a paper aeroplane, I could have sent Derek the message like this...

Avoiding
nosy kids like
Buster Jones

Derek

How to Make a Paper Aeroplane

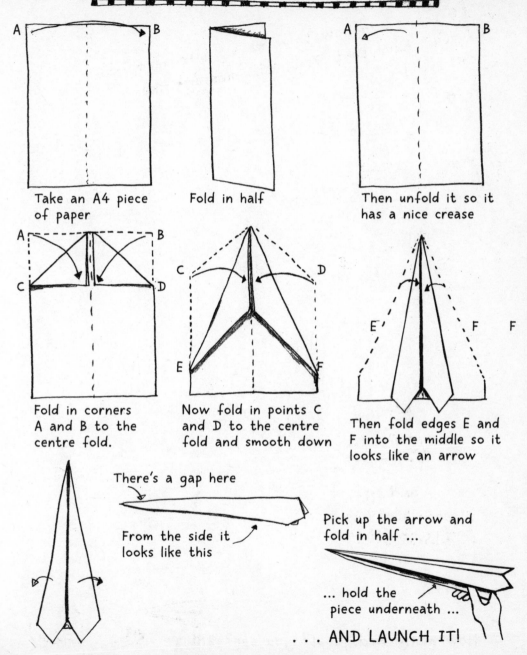

Take an A4 piece of paper

Fold in half

Then unfold it so it has a nice crease

Fold in corners A and B to the centre fold.

Now fold in points C and D to the centre fold and smooth down

Then fold edges E and F into the middle so it looks like an arrow

There's a gap here

From the side it looks like this

Pick up the arrow and fold in half ...

... hold the piece underneath ...

. . . AND LAUNCH IT!

How many birds could you see? 28!

For more news about the
Tom Gates books, go to
SCHOLASTIC'S FANTASTIC
Tom Gates website:

scholastic.ca/tomgates

When Liz was little, she loved to draw, paint and make things. Her mum used to say she was very good at making a mess (which is still true today!).

She kept drawing and went to art school, where she earned a degree in graphic design. She worked as a designer and art director in the music industry, and her freelance work has appeared on a wide variety of products.

Liz is the author-illustrator of several picture books. Tom Gates is the first series of books she has written and illustrated for older children. They have won several prestigious awards, including the Roald Dahl Funny Prize, the Waterstones Children's Book Prize, and the Blue Peter Book Award. The books have been translated into thirty-seven languages worldwide.

Mince is the same as ground meat. Slop...

 Oi! ≡ Hey!

Pudding ≡ dessert (all kinds — yum!)

 A REGISTER is the attendance book that the teacher would ✓ tick you off in, in the morning to make sure you're not LATE.

Rubbish ≡

Rumbled! basically means You're busted!

Garbage

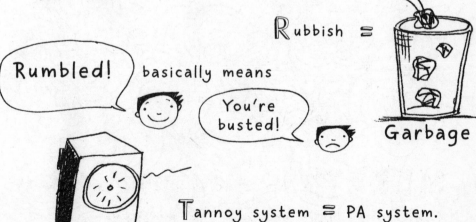

Tannoy system ≡ PA system.

12|5 LE BRICOLAGE

REGISTRE : usuel

ACTES DE COMMUNICATION PRINCIPAUX :
Demander/donner des informations ▶ B1/B2 — Dire ce qu'on aime/ce qu'on n'aime pas ▶ D10 — Dire qu'on a tort ▶ D5 — Dire qu'on est d'accord ▶ D4 — Demander à quelqu'un de faire quelque chose ▶ C1 — Proposer/Accepter un service ▶ C9/C10

Roger fait des petits travaux chez des particuliers.
Il sonne à l'appartement de Madame Laurier.

ROGER : Bonjour Madame. Vot'voisine Madame Bloch m'a dit que vous aviez une pièce à repeindre?

Mme LAURIER : Ah, oui. Elle m'a dit beaucoup de bien de vous, Monsieur.

ROGER : C'est gentil de sa part.

Mme LAURIER : Entrez Monsieur. Voilà la pièce.

ROGER : *Vous avez choisi la couleur?* (B1)

Mme LAURIER : *Les murs en beige... et le plafond en blanc naturellement.* (B2)

ROGER : *En mat ou en brillant?* (B1)

Mme LAURIER : *Mais en mat, bien sûr.* (B2) *Quelle horreur la peinture brillante!* (D10)

ROGER : *Bon, bon, je n'ai rien dit!* (D5) Enfin, *moi j'aime bien...* (D10)

Mme LAURIER : Alors, *vous me faites un devis?* (C1)

ROGER : *Peinture comprise?* (B1)

Mme LAURIER : *Mais bien entendu!* (D4) Je ne vais quand même pas acheter la peinture moi-même!

ROGER : *D'accord, d'accord!* (D4) Alors pour le travail, disons deux, trois jours. Ça vous fera entre mille cinq cents et deux mille francs. Pour la peinture, il faut que je vérifie au magasin. *Je vous téléphone ce soir?* (C9)

Mme LAURIER : *Oui.* (C10) Normalement je suis là.

ROGER : Alors, *je vous donnerai un devis précis à ce moment-là.* (C9)

Mme LAURIER : *Entendu.* (C10) Merci, Monsieur.

8|3   A LA DISCOTHÈQUE

REGISTRE : usuel/familier

ACTES DE COMMUNICATION PRINCIPAUX :

Inviter ▶ A7 — Refuser l'invitation ▶ A9 — Insister (réponse négative) ▶ B11 —
Dire ce qu'on préfère ▶ D13 — Demander une information ▶ B1 —
Gagner du temps pour réfléchir ▶ E5 — Se débarrasser de quelqu'un ▶ C29 —
Exprimer l'irritation ▶ D30

ÉRIC : (il s'approche d'une jeune fille assise) *Vous voulez danser?* (A7)

HÉLÈNE : *Non, merci.* (A9)

ÉRIC : Allez ! Pour une fois qu'il y a de la place sur la piste[1].

HÉLÈNE : *Non, vraiment.* (B11) *Je préfère rester assise.* (D13)

ÉRIC : (il voit une chaise inoccupée à côté d'Hélène) *Et cette place, elle est libre?* (B1)

HÉLÈNE : *Euh, c'est-à-dire,* (E5) je suis avec un copain. Il est allé me chercher à boire.

ÉRIC : Alors, on fait un petit tour de piste[2] en attendant qu'il revienne?

HÉLÈNE : *Écoutez, j'ai déjà dit non !* (B11) *Laissez-moi tranquille, s'il vous plaît !* (C29)

ÉRIC : Ça va ! Ça va ! J'ai compris ! (Il s'en va.) *Y en a marre*[3] (D30) des filles qui viennent pour rester assises !

1. La piste = l'endroit où l'on danse.
2. On fait un petit tour de piste = on danse un peu.
3. ○ Y en a marre = j'en ai assez...

2|3 UNE JEUNE FEMME SE PLAINT A SON PROPRIÉTAIRE

REGISTRE : usuel

ACTES DE COMMUNICATION PRINCIPAUX :
Demander à quelqu'un de faire quelque chose ▶ C1 — Dire qu'on est mécontent ▶ D7 — Dire sa surprise ▶ D22 — Insister ▶ B11 — Promettre ▶ C22 — Rassurer ▶ C23 — Dire qu'on est d'accord ▶ D4

NATHALIE : Bonjour, Monsieur Ruyer. Voici le loyer pour le mois prochain.

M. RUYER : Merci, Madame. Ça va?

NATHALIE : Eh bien, justement, *j'ai un petit problème.* (C1) Le chauffe-eau ne marche pas.

M. RUYER : Ah bon?

NATHALIE : *Est-ce que vous pourriez* (C1) demander à quelqu'un de venir jeter un coup d'œil?

M. RUYER : Ben[1]... Écoutez, *ça m'ennuie* (D7) d'envoyer un plombier si c'est pas vraiment en panne. *Ça m'étonne* (D22) qu'il ne marche pas, parce qu'il est neuf, hein[2]? Vous avez vérifié la veilleuse?

NATHALIE : Mais oui, bien sûr! *Je vous assure que* (B11) l'appareil est en panne. *Et ça m'agace* (D7) de ne pas avoir d'eau chaude!

M. RUYER : Bon, alors, *je vais essayer* (C22) de trouver quelqu'un. *Ne vous en faites pas!* (C23)

NATHALIE : Le plus tôt possible, hein?

M. RUYER : *D'accord! D'accord!* (D4) *C'est promis!* (C22) Au revoir, Madame.

1. ○ Ben = eh bien.
2. ○ Hein? = n'est-ce pas?

D|19 Dire sa déception

Dialogue : 3.4

▶ **Quand on est déçu par quelque chose :**

— *Alors, ce film, ça t'a plu ?*
— Non, j'ai été très déçu(e).
— Ça m'a (beaucoup) déçu(e).

▶ **Quand on est déçu par une promesse :**

— *Elle avait promis de m'écrire, mais ça fait des mois que je n'ai pas de nouvelles d'elle.*

— Elle m'a vraiment déçu(e).

— Je n'aurais pas cru | ça d'elle.
　　　　　　　　　　　| cela d'elle.

A RETENIR !

Quand on veut acheter quelque chose qui n'est pas disponible, ou qu'on ne peut obtenir, on peut dire « Tant pis ! ».

— Une baguette, s'il vous plaît.
— Il n'y en a plus, Madame.

— Tant pis. | (Alors donnez-moi...)
　　　　　　 | (Est-ce qu'il y a une autre boulangerie dans le coin ?)

« Tant pis ! » n'est pas une expression impolie : elle exprime l'acceptation d'un fait.

D|20 Dire sa peur/ ses craintes/son soulagement

Dialogues : 11.3 : 11.4 ; 12.3

▶ **Pour exprimer une peur physique :**

— J'ai très peur (des examens, de prendre l'avion.)
☐ — Je crains (la foule, l'altitude.)
○ — J'ai la frousse[1].
○ — J'ai une de ces trouilles[2] !

1. ○ Avoir la frousse = avoir peur.
2. ○ Avoir la trouille = avoir peur.

C|26 Rappeler quelque chose à quelqu'un

Dialogues : 6.2 ; 6.4

▶ **Si quelqu'un a oublié, ou risque d'oublier un rendez-vous, un devoir... :**

- Je te rappelle que (qu')
- N'oublie pas que (qu')
- Tu te souviens que (qu')
- Dis-donc, tu n'oublies pas que (qu')
- Si j'ai bonne mémoire,
- Il me semble bien que (qu')

(tu me dois 50 dollars.)
(on a rendez-vous avec le prof cet après-midi.)
(la réunion de ce soir est reportée à jeudi.)

▶ **Quand on a demandé quelque chose et que l'autre personne n'a pas réagi, n'a pas entendu ou semble avoir oublié :**

Devant un guichet. Dans un café...

— Je m'excuse de vous déranger, mais j'ai demandé...

— Dites, on a demandé... Vous n'avez pas oublié?

— Dites donc, j'ai demandé... | Vous voulez bien me le donner? Vous n'avez pas entendu?

▶**Quand on connaît la personne :**

- Dis-donc, je t'ai dit qu' (il fallait se dépêcher.)
- Tu n'oublies pas que (c'est ton tour pour la vaisselle?)

ATTENTION!

Il est très important de distinguer les différents sens du verbe « devoir », qui peut indiquer :

1. L'obligation morale, la nécessité :
   - Je dois lui rendre ce livre avant demain.
   - Il est arrivé en retard. J'ai dû attendre une demi-heure.

2. Une forte probabilité :
   - Tu le vois ?
   - Non, mais normalement, il doit être là. (= Il est probablement là.) (= Je suis presque certain(e) qu'il est là.)
   - Comment, elle est déjà là ?
   - Oui, elle a dû partir avant la fin de son cours. (= Elle est sans doute partie avant la fin de son cours.) (= Je suis presque certain(e) qu'elle est partie avant la fin de son cours.)

En général, le contexte indique le sens.

▶ **La possibilité :**
- Tu crois (qu'il sait ?)
     - C'est bien possible.
- Peut-être que (qu') (il fera beau demain).
- (Il fera beau demain) peut-être.
- ☐ - Il se peut que (qu') | (il fasse beau demain).
- - Il se pourrait que (qu') |

ATTENTION!

« Paraître » est un verbe très fréquemment employé pour exprimer la possibilité. Mais, il a deux sens bien distincts selon la structure utilisée :
   - Il paraît malade. (= Il a l'air malade).
   - Il paraît qu'il est malade.   (= On dit qu'il est malade).
   ○ - Paraît qu'il est malade.

ATTENTION!

Quand vous refusez une offre à boire, un deuxième verre, ou si vous ne voulez plus reprendre du plat servi, votre hôte (hôtesse) va sans doute, par politesse, insister :

– Allez, juste un tout petit peu !
– Vous êtes sûr(e)? Vous n'en voulez plus?
– Mais vous n'avez pas beaucoup mangé!...

Vous pouvez dire :

– Non, vraiment, c'est | très bon | mais j'ai très bien mangé.
| délicieux | mais je n'ai plus faim.
– Merci, mais vraiment, | je n'en veux plus.
| j'ai très bien mangé.

Ce qu'il ne faut pas dire :

– Ne traduisez pas des expressions de votre langue maternelle telles que « Je suis plein(e) » ; cette expression est totalement inappropriée.
– Ne dites pas « J'en ai assez », qui peut traduire l'irritation et l'exaspération.

$\overline{A}|18$ Faire un compliment

Dialogue : 6.3

Un compliment fait plaisir, et crée une bonne ambiance. Toutefois, il vaut mieux le réserver à des gens qu'on connaît bien.

Voici quelques compliments que l'on peut faire :

– Vous avez bonne mine aujourd'hui. (= Vous avez l'air en forme.)
– J'aime bien tes cheveux comme ça.
– Quelle jolie robe !
– Elle te va bien, cette robe !
– Qu'est-ce qu'elle est | belle, ta montre !
○ | chouette, ta montre !

When it's over, Mr Fullerman tells us we'll find out how we did at...

PARENTS' EVENING

(Like that's something to look forward to.)

"Nothing to worry about at all," he adds.

PLAN A b c d e F G h I j K L
M n O P Q r s t U V W x Y

(I've lost track.)

Z

Me, Derek, Norman, Solid and Brad are all hanging out together in the school grounds after the TEST.

"I'm glad THAT'S over," Norman says.

"Me too," I agree. Then Derek asks me if I've worked out my SPEECH for the **school council election...**